THE PRINCETON REVIEW

Research Paper
Smart

THE PRINCETON REVIEW

Research Paper Smart

WHERE TO FIND IT, HOW TO WRITE IT, HOW TO CITE IT

BY LIZ BUFFA

RANDOM HOUSE, INC.
New York 1997
http://www.randomhouse.com

Princeton Review Publishing, L.L.C.
2315 Broadway
New York, NY 10024
E-mail: info@review.com

Copyright © 1997 by Princeton Review Publishing, L.L.C.

ISBN 0-679-78382-2

Editor: Lesly Atlas
Designer: Illeny Maaza
Production Editor: James Petrozzello
Production Coordinator: Matthew Reilly

Manufactured in the United States of America on recycled paper.

9 8 7 6 5 4 3 2 1

First Edition

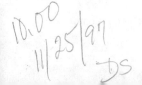

ACKNOWLEDGMENTS

The author wishes to thank Jeannie Yoon and Evan Schnittman for their support and Lesly Atlas for her editing expertise. Thanks also go to James Petrozzello, Matthew Reilly, Rich Klin, Maria Russo, and Marcia Lerner fo their additional creative input.

Thanks once again to Marcia Lerner and Dominick Buffa for everything else.

CONTENTS

Introduction

WHY BE RESEARCH PAPER SMART?

Most students tremble at the thought of a research project. It seems that the amount of trembling is directly proportional to the length of the paper assigned. A two- or three-page paper might seem bad enough, but problems increase exponentially as you approach twenty pages, thirty pages, and even longer papers.

Fortunately, there's a way out of this for you, the reader of this book. We plan to take you through the research process, from its very inception—picking a topic—to the finer points of its presentation. All of this will be done in the simplest, most direct manner. Don't worry. Figuring out how to write a research paper will be less troublesome than the task of writing the paper.

Actually, writing a research paper can be relatively painless and useful. You will find that, like many things in life, there is a difficult way and an easy way. In this case, the easy way is best. Believe it or not, learning to research properly and to write a paper is useful in many aspects of life. You might one day find yourself sitting behind a desk having to read through reports and summarize them. What's that? It's research! Lawyers need to do research all the time. There are many fields in which research and writing skills are extremely useful. So, stop thinking you can just do a halfway decent job in college and that you will never have to do this again.

You will find that the only thing you feared is the unknown. Perhaps you have never really used a library, or you have never had to write footnotes. These things may be intimidating, but we will make them easy.

WHAT IS A RESEARCH PAPER?

Let's begin by giving a simple definition for a research paper. Your teachers might be asking you to write "a report," "a term paper," or even just "a paper" on a subject. Are these research papers? Are we talking about the same thing? These terms are all quite vague, and there is no set definition for each, but we'll give you a brief example of what is usually considered acceptable for each of the following types of assignments. To illustrate, we will take a simple subject: George Washington.

REPORT

If an instructor asked you to write a report on George Washington, most likely he would expect you to read some general information about George Washington and present the material you have learned in written form. You would demonstrate to your professor that you have done the reading required for the class, as well as some outside reading. You would not be expected to go beyond basic sources (textbooks or reference works), or find out anything startling or new about George Washington.

PERSUASIVE ESSAY

A persuasive essay is usually quite short (perhaps a page or two). Its purpose is to persuade a reader of a particular point of view. If you were asked to write a persuasive essay about

George Washington, it might have a title like "George Washington: Our Greatest President." To present a reader with an argument for George Washington's greatness, you would use some of the information gleaned from basic sources read in the course. You must find facts that support your point of view, but, unless you are asked to do so, you do not necessarily have to find contradictory sources.

PERSONAL ESSAY

Personal essays are also usually quite short, and are frequently assigned in writing classes. You are not expected to do research for a personal essay. Here, you are simply relating some personal experience. A professor might require you to write a personal essay relating your grade school instruction on George Washington. This might be a useful way to discuss some of the myths and misinformation children are taught.

TERM PAPER

A term paper is a broad category, into which many types of papers might fall. It is usually a final paper for a course. Its form will vary depending on the course and the teacher. A term paper is not necessarily a long research paper.

REVIEW OF THE LITERATURE

This is most similar to a report. If you were studying George Washington in your introduction to political science course, you might be asked to read several different sources and summarize each. A "review of the literature" assignment allows you to demonstrate that you understand the basic information presented in each source. Typically, you will include a "review of the literature" as part of a full research paper or thesis.

RESEARCH PAPER

A traditional research paper goes beyond all of the above in scope. First of all, you are typically looking to find out something you didn't know before. A research paper about George Washington might set out to prove that George Washington was not a great general, but only won the American War for Independence because the British were incompetent. You would seek out many different sources to support your idea or thesis. You are expected to do more than just summarize what you read; you are expected to draw conclusions from it.

THESES AND DISSERTATIONS

These are the most advanced forms of research writing. Thesis work generally refers to a high caliber of detailed research conducted on a graduate level, or on the undergraduate level in a senior honors class. A dissertation is a book-length report that culminates years of research on a topic. It is the completion of the doctoral degree and, as such, must conform to the most rigorous standards of research and writing.

We will go into more detail in later chapters about how to work on many types of papers. However, as you can see, different papers require different things from the writer. Your professor will spell out in detail the type of paper you are writing, or she will expect you to ask. The first lesson is: Always consult your professor about any lingering questions you may have. No book can answer questions about a teacher's expectations.

WHY SHOULD PAPERS CONFORM TO CERTAIN STYLES?

There will certainly be some point in your research and writing when you throw your hands up at the absurdity of it all. Why bother with nitpicky footnotes? Who cares if the commas are here and the periods are there? Why can't I write things in my own style? These are legitimate questions. It may appear to you that professors are a bunch of sadists whose only joy is getting students to fret over arcane points of style and grammar.

The primary goal of writing is communication. While you may be more relaxed about points of style in your speech, you need to be exact in written communication. Good writing is precise and clear. Don't confuse using a lot of big words with being a good writer. Learning about how to style a paper properly will help you learn how to communicate clearly. Using standard notation for things like footnotes and bibliography entries enables your teacher to identify your outside sources and see that you have cited them correctly.

It bears repeating: The process of writing a research paper will be rewarding and useful in many different areas throughout your life. *Research Paper Smart* is designed to make that process as smooth as possible.

HOW THIS BOOK IS ORGANIZED

The order of topics in *Research Paper Smart* is designed to follow, chronologically, the steps you need to go through in writing a research paper. If you've already been assigned a topic, you can skip the first section about finding and narrowing down your research topic.

If, however, this is the very beginning of your first real research paper, then start at the beginning and use each section to guide you through the process.

Getting Started

1

Of a good beginning, cometh a good end.

John Heywood

Perhaps the most difficult part of any project is getting started. The broader the range of topics in front of you, the more difficult it is to begin. The starting point, however, is one of the most critical points of your research project. Embarking down the path of research on a topic that offers little or no information will be among the most frustrating tasks you can imagine. A good topic is like a good book—always satisfying and challenging.

FINDING AND CLARIFYING YOUR TOPIC

In many classes, you'll never need to worry about finding a topic for your research paper—it will be provided for you. Many teachers like to assign one topic for the class, or to give a list of assignments that you must choose from. If your professor does not assign a topic, your first job is to find one.

You may think that the thing to do is to pick a topic that you find interesting. While you do want to have interest in the topic, it is equally important to find one on which you can conduct research. While you may have always wondered about the nocturnal habits of the animals of Ndola, if there is no scholarly work on the subject, you will be in trouble. So your first job is to select a broad category. Perhaps it will be dictated by the nature of the course you are taking. If not, you may consider one of the following sources:

- Personal experience

- Peer groups (network with friends to discuss areas of interest)

- Topics in the news

- Your course syllabus

- Table of contents for the standard text in your course

- Bibliography for the standard text in your course

- *The Reader's Guide to Periodical Literature*

- An encyclopedia

- A librarian

You want to find a topic that has three important characteristics:

- It is of interest to you.

- There appears to be a lot of information available on this topic.

- You have the background or expertise to understand and write about the information you'll be reading.

While the first point—your interest in the topic—is very important, the latter two are not to be underestimated. Avoid picking difficult science topics, for example, if you have little science background. You will be stuck reading articles that you cannot possibly comprehend, and trying to compose a paper that is beyond your grasp. The only alternative will be to refer to sources that treat your subject superficially, which would make for an unacceptable paper.

Once you have chosen a broad category, you will need to narrow the scope. We will use the following broad category as an example:

Art

Now, you need to continually narrow down your subject area. For example,

Art

Painting

Impressionism

Claude Monet

As you can see, we've progressed from a comprehensive topic, *Art*, to a type of art—painting—to a style of painting—Impressionism—to one artist who practiced that style of painting—Claude Monet. Still, there is quite a bit of information available about Claude Monet. If you're unfamiliar with the subject, how can you narrow down this topic even further? One of the easiest ways is to consult an encyclopedia. Most professors do *not* consider the encyclopedia a valid source for a legitimate academic study, but it does, however, have its use as a general introduction to a subject. For example, if you consulted the entry for *Art* in a standard encyclopedia, at the end of the article you would find a *see also* or *related topics* entry. Some of the related topics for *Art* might be:

Styles of *Art*

Baroque

Classicism

Gothic Art

Impressionism

Surrealism

You might decide after reading the entry for *Art* that Impressionism interests you. Look up *Impressionism* and the general introduction will tell you that the leading French impressionists were Manet, Pissarro, Degas, Sisley, Monet, and Renoir. Zip over to the *M* volume and look up Monet. Here, you could read a brief biography of Claude Monet and find references to other sources written on the artist.

Another great way to narrow down your topic is to use a Web-based search engine. We will discuss how to use them in this chapter's section on the Internet.

This process is the first step in narrowing down your topic. But now, you need to narrow it down even more. The first thing to consider is the length of your assignment. Do you need to write a three-page paper or a twenty-page paper? Even if you were going to write a biographical sketch of Monet, you'd probably need to concentrate on a specific part of his life. This greater clarification will usually come from reading more into the subject. Your next step will be to move past the encyclopedia and on to other sources of information.

GATHERING PRELIMINARY INFORMATION

The process of gathering preliminary information is one that students often rush through. While you may not find out anything of great import, these early stages will be the key to leading you in the right direction and laying the foundation of knowledge you need to conduct proper research. Your goal when doing preliminary research is to:

- Find out enough about your subject to ascertain whether or not this is a topic you could write about easily.

- Find out how much information is available about your subject, and what kind of information is available. In other words, will you be able to find enough scholarly work about your topic? (No, *People* magazine profiles do not count.)

- Write an outline.

- Construct your thesis statement, if necessary.

TYPES OF RESEARCH

There are several types of research that you might conduct. Thinking about the structure of your research may help you in these early stages to give form to your inquiry.

HISTORICAL RESEARCH

In this case, you want to use historical documents to reconstruct an incident or review evidence about something that took place in the past. Think of historical research as piecing together a very old puzzle.

CASE STUDY RESEARCH

This type of research is widely used in scientific (including economic, political, and social science) study. Here, you might investigate several different related case studies. These studies provide information about a subject or series of subjects. After examining the different cases, you draw conclusions from the information you have found. A typical case study research paper might address the effects of price fluctuations on different buyers, or the effects of a certain medical treatment on different patients.

DEVELOPMENTAL RESEARCH

This is a timeline sort of research. You investigate how a problem or situation develops over a period of time. Your goal is to find the order or pattern underlying the development and to draw a conclusion based on that. An example of developmental research would be to investigate the impact of a new law in an area over a period of one year.

These are just a few of the types of research you may wish to explore. Naturally there are many different ways to conduct research; these are simply some suggestions.

EVALUATING SOURCE MATERIAL AND FINDING YOUR LIBRARY'S RESOURCES

If you have not done so already, you should start familiarizing yourself with your library's catalog. This will be the first place of inquiry in any research you will have to do in your education. Most libraries today have some sort of online catalog, with its own catchy name. The online catalogs at the New York Public Library are called CATNYP (CATalog of the New York Public) and LEO (Library Entrance Online). Most online or public access catalogs allow the patron to search the library's catalogs in the following ways:

- **Author** search. If you know the name of the author, you can enter it and search for a specific book. If you know that a particular person has written extensively on a subject, but are uncertain what the titles of his or her books are, this is the most efficient way to search.

- **Title** search. This allows you to enter the title of the book, and find out its location, even if you are not sure of the author's name.

- **Subject** search. You can find all the books listed on a given subject by conducting a subject search. You may, however, need to narrow your search further when using this technique. (See "Conducting a Search," below.)

- **Keyword** search. This search is most useful if you're not exactly sure of a book's title, but you know enough to enter a keyword from the title or the subject. Say, for example, you want to look up the book *Monet at Giverny*, but cannot remember the full title. Either keywords, *Monet* or *Giverny*, should locate the book if it is at your library.

The great advantage of using online catalogs is that they are usually able to give you more information than a regular card catalog. Many will tell you not only where the book is located and its full title and author, but also whether it is in circulation, and if so, when it is due back at the library. An online catalog may also give information about other libraries, or tell you if your library has borrowing privileges with another.

Card Catalogs

Even if your library has an online catalog, it may use a card catalog for the older works in its collection. Typically, libraries began to go online in the early 1980s. Therefore, there may be books from the period that predated the online catalog that are not indexed there. So you should be familiar with the card catalog as well. Consult the online information sheets or the librarian to find out the parameters of the online catalog.

The card catalog at most libraries is usually set up in one of three ways:

> It is divided into three parts: subject, author, and title catalogs,
>
> or
>
> It is integrated, with subject, author, and title cards all mixed in one large catalog,
>
> or
>
> It is partially integrated with author and title cards in one catalog and subject cards in another.

When you locate information, either in the card catalog or in the online catalog, you will discover where in the library the book is located, *and* exactly where to find it on the shelves. Many universities have more than one library, so be sure you know where to look. You don't want to waste time in the science library if the book you are looking for is back in the main library.

How do you know if the information you are finding is acceptable? There are many different checkpoints:

1. Who is the publisher? It is a well-respected publisher or an academic press? If you do not recognize the publisher, ask your librarian if the publisher is a reputable one.

2. Who is the author? Check out the credentials of the author and/or editorial board of the work. What are the academic affiliations or previous published works?

3. When was the source published? It may be fine to use source material from 1953, as long as the information has not changed. Population statistics or geographical boundaries need to be verified by using sources that are updated frequently. If you are examining an Internet resource, check to see how frequently the page is updated.

4. What are the bibliographic sources cited? The more scholarly the information, the better the bibliographic citations will be. Popular magazines typically don't cite sources at all.

5. If the source is a periodical, is it indexed in a reputable index or abstract (see below)? Journals will only be indexed if they are considered to be respected in the field.

These are just some of the concerns you should have when you verify source material. Always check your sources and make sure you aren't using and citing bad information. When in doubt, ask either your teacher or librarian.

CLASSIFICATION SYSTEMS

Books are classified in one of two ways: Library of Congress classification or Dewey decimal classification. For the most part, academic libraries use the Library of Congress classification and public libraries use the Dewey decimal system. The Library of Congress classification uses a combination of letters and numbers. There are twenty main subject divisions:

A. General works

B. Philosophy, psychology, and religion

C. General history

D. World history

E-F. American history

G. Geography and anthropology

H. Social sciences

J. Political science

K. Law

L. Education

M. Music

N. Fine arts

P. Language and literature

Q. Science

R. Medicine

S. Agriculture

T. Technology

U. Military science

V. Naval science

Z. Bibliography and library science

The Dewey decimal system has ten main subject categories:

000 General works

100 Philosophy and psychology

200 Religion

300 Social Sciences

400 Language

500 Natural sciences and mathematics

600 Technology and applied sciences

700 Fine arts

800 Literature

900 Geography and history

Within each broad-subject heading, there are subcategory breakdowns. For example, a history of world literature is classified under 809, and nineteenth-century world literature would be classified under 809.034.

You do not need to memorize the classification systems at your library. It doesn't hurt to be familiar with them, but the idea of classification is that you can find things even if you are not sure of all the categories. Just look them up. Grouping a collection by subject will be useful if you like to browse the stacks once you have a call letter. Then, you can go to the section, find your book, and take a look at the books around it on the shelves. Chances are they may be of interest to you as well.

GENERAL REFERENCE SOURCES

These days, with the general inclination to conduct research using electronic resources, it is easy for a student to forget some of the basic reference sources that have served students so well for many years. These general sources are invaluable. Many of them do have electronic counterparts, but we still believe in the great process of leafing through volumes of reference sources in an attempt to familiarize yourself with a subject. The great problem with electronic research is that you pretty much lose the serendipitous find—looking through a volume for one subject and coming upon another that happens to be nearby.

The purpose of the general reference sources we will discuss is to gather preliminary information on your subject, and to inject your paper with facts, definitions and general information that will enhance your own theories.

Encyclopedias

There are many different types of encyclopedias. Although most general ones, as we've said before, are not really appropriate for academic research, they are good starting points. You are probably familiar with the *World Book Encyclopedia*, *The Encyclopedia Brittanica*, *The Encyclopedia Americana*, and *Collier's*, for example. Most libraries will have a variety of encyclopedias and you should consult them if you are unfamiliar with your subject.

What you may not realize is that there are a number of specialized encyclopedias that are a sort of middle ground. They contain a greater number of subjects in their respective fields and explore them in greater depth. Here is a list of some of the more popular specialized encyclopedias you are likely to find in your library. While this is not a complete list, it is intended to give you some ideas for more in-depth preliminary research. Their titles pretty much explain the subject range of information to be found within:

- *Encyclopedia of Sociology*

- *Encyclopedia of the American Presidency*

- *McGraw-Hill Encyclopedia of Science and Technology*

- *Encyclopedia of American Forest and Conservation History*

- *Encyclopedia of Social Work*

- *Encyclopedia of World Art*

- *Encyclopedia of Asian History*

- *Harvard Encyclopedia of American Ethnic Groups*

Dictionaries

Though we are separating dictionaries into a separate category from encyclopedias, they serve similar purposes. There are as many different dictionaries as there are encyclopedias—from single-volume ready reference sources, to multivolume works that you may use as part of your more extensive research.

What probably pops into your head when you hear the term *dictionary* is a standard reference book you use to look up the definition of a word. Dictionaries may go into much more depth and be useful when researching the etymology of a term (how it came into being), or important style and usage points.

The most commonly used dictionaries are the *Random House Dictionary*, *Merriam-Webster's New Collegiate Dictionary*, and *Webster's New Universal*. The more academic version of these is the *Oxford English Dictionary*, or *OED*. The *OED* is a multivolume dictionary that gives the history of each word—showing its usage as far back as early English literature. Here, you may discover the first recorded time that a word was ever used—say, in a Shakespearean play or Chaucer's *Canterbury Tales*. Many of the entries are pages long and give valuable usage and historical information.

Other dictionaries that are more specialized include:

- *Black's Law Dictionary*

- *Partridge's Dictionary of Slang*

- *New Palgrave Dictionary of Economics*

- *The New Grove Dictionary of Music and Musicians (much more an encyclopedia in both scope and length)*

- *Dorland's Illustrated Medical Dictionary*

- *The Dorling-Kindersley Visual Dictionary*

Statistical Sources and Fact Books

These range from ready reference books, such as the *World Almanac*, to detailed statistical sources. The biggest publisher of statistical information is the United States government. The plethora of government statistics can be very difficult to make your way through. Keep in mind that reference librarians can be of great help in accomplishing this task. Use the following references to seek statistics and facts that will support your work and enhance your paper's worth.

Britannia Book of the Year is a yearly supplement to the *Encyclopedia Britannica*. It contains information about newsworthy events of the year. Use it to update information you have researched that may be dated. Also, don't forget to check out previous yearbooks for historical information on your topic. Most encyclopedias publish yearbooks—they can be very useful reference tools.

World Almanac and Book of Facts, published annually by the Newspaper Enterprise Association since 1868, is a wonderful quick source for statistical and news information. Do you need to verify who Franklin Delano Roosevelt's second vice president was? Perhaps you need to know about the gross national product of a certain country. The World Almanac is updated yearly, but older copies are excellent for historical research.

Facts on File: Weekly World News Digest with Cumulative Index is updated weekly with factual current events. It is an excellent place to verify statistics and information. Cumulative indexes are published every five years.

Vertical File Index, published by H.W. Wilson, is an index to pamphlets and booklets—the kind that are kept in the vertical files of your library. The reference librarian may have his own vertical-file index to clippings and files of local interest. Ask for it, especially if the library you are working in may have special information on your subject (for example, if it is in the home-town of a person in your report).

The Statistical Abstract of the United States is an annual publication of the United States Bureau of the Census that has a great deal of demographic and census information.

Statistical Yearbook and *Demographic Yearbook* are other valuable sources of information and are published by the United Nations every year.

Atlases and Gazetteers

Atlases are collections of maps and gazetteers are books of geographic information. Whether you need to know a specific location or population or find an illustration for a report, you should be familiar with how to use these reference tools. Atlases usually have a comprehensive index to place-names that will reference a map and location on that map. Gazetteers are usually arranged alphabetically by place-name.

The National Atlas of the United States, The Times Atlas of the World, and *The Rand McNally Universal World Atlas* are among the most popular atlases. *The Columbia Lippincott Gazetteer of the World* is one of the premier gazetteers available.

CONDUCTING A SEARCH

Whether you are searching an online catalog in your library, or conducting an expensive search on Lexis/Nexis, you need to know a little about how to search.

There are many different types of databases, and knowing how to search properly will save you a good deal of time. Doing an efficient search is especially important if you are paying for your access time, or if your library limits online time. Here are some general guidelines and terms for you to be familiar with.

Boolean Searching

When you first begin a search, you may try using general search terms, looking for a rough subject category that will match yours. If, for example, you are considering research on

Theodore Roosevelt's tenure as New York's police commissioner, you may try general terms like *Roosevelt*. You can imagine the number of entries that would return if you typed that in! Some databases allow you to narrow your search using what is called Boolean operators, or the words AND, OR, and NOT. Boolean operators are typed in capital letters. Here's how it works:

Roosevelt AND police AND commissioner would find entries that contain all of these words only. This would eliminate entries about Roosevelt as president of the United States.

Police OR commissioner would locate articles about either the police or commissioners. It will also pick up articles that contain both words. The OR search will locate many more entries than the AND search. It is most practical when you need to enlarge your search fields because your preliminary search yielded few good results.

Roosevelt NOT Franklin will pick up any articles about a Roosevelt who is not Franklin Roosevelt. This kind of search is useful when you notice that your search repeatedly renders information associated with someone or something else. For example, if you were investigating Monet, and kept finding articles about the sales of his paintings at auction, you might use the search "Monet NOT auction."

You may combine searching techniques thus:

Roosevelt AND (police OR commissioner). This will bring up entries that contain the word *Roosevelt*, but only if they also contain either *police* or *commissioner*, or both.

Wild Card Searching

Some databases allow you to use what is called a wild card search. This is helpful if you're not entirely sure of the spelling of a term, or if you want to call up a variety of terms that have different endings. You may use an asterisk (*) as a "wild card," meaning that it could stand for anything. Say, for example, you are trying to search for articles about psychology, but are coming up short. Using the wild card search, you may enter:

psycholog*

This will bring up entries with the key words *psychology*, *psychologists*, *psychological*, and so on.

Wild card searching is a great way to ensure that you're not missing out on entries because they contain commonly abbreviated words. Suppose you want to find out about an event that took place in Dallas in November. Using the search:

Dallas AND November

may eliminate your finding anything in which November is abbreviated Nov. Try the wild card search:

Dallas AND Nov*

This will return items that contain both November and Nov. in combination with Dallas.

TIP

If you are having trouble finding information on your subject, make sure your spelling is correct.

BEYOND THE CARD CATALOG AND GENERAL REFERENCE WORKS

While your card catalog is a good place to start, there are many other places to search. The library catalog does not contain all the information about the holdings in the library.

The following are other equally, if not more, important places to search.

Periodicals

Periodicals, because they come out on a regular basis, contain information that is far more up-to-date than that which is contained in books. If your research is truly academic, you need to do some periodical research to find out what is happening in the field you are investigating. There are two main types of periodicals: magazines and journals.

Magazines typically contain articles of general interest. Some of the most popular magazines are:

- *Time*
- *Newsweek*
- *People*
- *U.S. News & World Report*
- *Science News*
- *BusinessWeek*

These magazines have a general audience and do not, as a rule, cite sources. They typically contain glossy photos and report on broad topics.

Journals, on the other hand, cater to a select field. They are not intended to be read by a general audience and, as such, most are probably unfamiliar to you if you are just starting research in your field. Journal articles, usually written by scholars in the field, will always cite sources. Examples of frequently referenced journals include:

- *Journal of the American Medical Association*

- *Studies in Romanticism*

- *Human Development*

- *Women's Studies International*

Not exactly the kind of stuff you'd pick up at your corner newsstand, eh? Most professors will frown on research that cites more magazines than journals. Journals are the more respected source in a research paper. This is not to say that it is never appropriate to use magazine research. Look at the following examples:

David, a senior, is writing a thesis on the dangers of a Western diet to immigrants from Eastern countries. He is consulting a number of scholarly journals about the latest studies being conducted around the world.

Paul, a freshman, is writing a paper for his expository writing class about his adventures on different low-fat diets. He consults a few popular magazines for examples of the latest fad diets.

As you can see, the trick is to find the source that is appropriate for the type of paper you are writing.

Periodical Searching

There are two types of places to search for periodicals: indexes and abstracts. An abstract gives a summary of the information found in each article; an index just lists the name of the article. There are printed indexes and abstracts as well as computerized, or online, forms of them.

Some of the More Popular Printed Indexes and Abstracts

While this is by no means a complete list of the indexes and abstracts available, it should give you a general idea of the range of information available. The list moves from the most general, popular indexes to the more exclusive, academic ones. Most indexes use some set of abbreviations for the magazines or journals they index. Be sure to check the front of the index for a key to the abbreviations or acronyms.

Reader's Guide to Periodical Literature

By far the most well-recognized periodical index, *The Reader's Guide to Periodical Literature* is introduced to most students in high school. It is like an encyclopedia in that it helps you narrow down your topic and learn basic information about the subject, yet it is not really the best tool for advanced research. The magazines indexed in *The Reader's Guide* are general popular magazines, such as *Time, Newsweek,* and *BusinessWeek*. The more academic, scholarly journals are not indexed here. While this is a good place for you to start, it should probably not be the only place you look.

Periodical Abstracts

Like the *Reader's Guide, Periodical Abstracts* covers a broad range of subject areas, but will also give you a brief summary of each article as well.

The New York Times /The Wall Street Journal/ The Christian Science Monitor Index

These are three of the most common indexes to three of the most influential papers in the United States. Any major news item can be found indexed in one of these three places.

Humanities Index

As the name implies, this indexes a number of journals that cover topics in the humanities, namely art, literature, criticism, music, and the like.

General Science Index

Here you will find indexed those journals dealing with biology, math, physics, medicine, and so on.

Social Sciences Index

Social sciences, such as anthropology, psychology, law, and current-events issues are found here. Most societal issues (homelessness, latchkey children, etc.) can be researched with the journals indexed here.

Resources in Education (RIE) and Current Index to Journals in Education (CIJE)

These indexes, sponsored by the United States Department of Education, correspond to the online database *ERIC (Education Resources Information Center)*. They are the best sources for any research on educational topics.

Biography Index

Indexes biographical material from over 2,700 periodicals, books (individual biographies and biography collections), and juvenile literature.

Essay and General Literature Index

Although this index is included here with the periodical indexes, it does not index periodicals per se, but essays and articles that are found in book anthologies and collections. The emphasis is on material that deals primarily with the arts and social sciences.

Index to Legal Periodicals

As the name implies, this is the place to look if you are doing any research on a law-related topic.

Biological Abstracts/Mathematical Reviews/Sociological Abstracts/Historical Abstracts

As you can see by the titles above, each of the more general abstracts (such as the *General Science Index*) is broken down in even more detail with its own subject index. Each of these titles contains information indexed from even more arcane academic journals in its field, as well as research that's being done all over the world. *Biological Abstracts*, for example, indexes and abstracts about 7,000 journals from over 90 countries.

Electronic Indexes, Abstracts, and Databases

Many of the indexes above have electronic or online counterparts that may be more efficient to search. Online searching allows you to move from one subject heading to another without having to move from volume to volume, or back and forth within a volume. Electronic indexes may also have the advantage of being updated more frequently and containing more information. Many electronic indexes have full text citations—in other words, you can actually call up the article if the citation looks interesting to you.

Once again, we are listing these electronic indexes in rough order from most general to most specific. This is not a comprehensive list, but it should give you an idea of the scope of indexes available.

InfoTrac. The *InfoTrac* system archives a variety of journals and magazines on a computer database. Conducting a search on the *InfoTrac* system will give you article citations, some with abstracts and some with full-text entries. There may be four separate databases in the *InfoTrac* system:

1. *Expanded Academic Index.* This covers a wide variety of liberal-arts subject categories. Social sciences, arts, science, current news, book reviews, and literary criticism are some of the subjects catalogued.

2. *General Business File ASAP.* Consolidated investment reports, corporate profiles, general business news, etc. are found on this database.

3. *Health Index ASAP.* Health and medical subjects.

4. *Magazine Index Plus.* This is the most popular database, on which most popular magazines are indexed. It is a good general database with subjects like travel, current events, general business, and entertainment. It does not index any real scholarly journals.

Periodical Abstracts. The online version of the previously listed print abstract.

Article First. Indexes the table of contents of each issue of more than 11,500 periodicals.

MLA Bibliography. Indexes over 3000 academic journals, series, and monographs on linguistics, literature, and folklore.

This is the online version of the *MLA International Bibliography of Books and Articles.*

Cumulative Book Index. Allows you to search the author, title or subject for books published in the English language.

Dissertation Abstracts International (DAI). Brief summaries of dissertations from over 500 universities and institutions of higher learning around the world. These abstracts date from the late nineteenth-century to the present.

GPO Access. Legislative, regulatory, and economic information. Contains many full-text citations from the federal government: bills, legislation, and *The Federal Register.*

Compact Disclosure. Financial and management information on more than 10,000 publicly owned companies. Information is gathered from the United States Securities and Exchange Commission.

BioethicsLine. Literature on the subject of ethics as it pertains to medicine, nursing, philosophy, law, and the like. This indexes and abstracts popular and academic sources: newspapers, monographs, bills, and journals, just to name a few.

These lists should give you an idea of the great variety of information indexed and abstracted in your library. Most libraries have a list of all their indexes. You should ask for it and take a look. If you've only done cursory research, you have no idea of what is available.

So, what next? You find a citation in your index, and now you need to find the actual source material. First of all, check to see if the database you are searching has a full-text version of the citation. Many do. If not, check with the librarian to see if they have the magazine or journal. If your library does not have a bound volume of the publication, you may need to request it and view it on CD-ROM or microfilm.

LEXIS/NEXIS, BRS, AND DIALOG

These are vast collections of databases. They are used extensively in many professions—journalism, law, and financial services, just to name a few. These databases may include the full text of many publications, which you may print out. The databases are extremely current and authoritative. They also charge for use. Some universities have an agreement to permit students to use them as long as the research is strictly course-related. Because of the strict regulation of the use of these expensive databases, most colleges will insist that users undergo some training before using them.

CD-ROM

CD-ROM stands for compact disc read-only memory. Like an audio compact disc, it can store a great deal of information in a compact, relatively permanent way. It has an advantage over microfilm in that it can store color images and sound and can be searched. Many of the indexes and statistical databases we have already reviewed are stored on CD-ROM. The 1990 Census, for example, is published in print and on CD-ROM. Because of its sometimes unwieldy statistical information, the CD-ROM can greatly ease the burden of finding a number.

While most users are familiar with CD-ROMs as indexes, they are also quite useful for multimedia exhibits. From general encyclopedias to more detailed texts, CD-ROMs may offer great enhancements to their print counterparts. You may be able to view a film clip, hear a speech, or see a painting. CD-ROMs may allow you to move around from reference to reference with greater ease.

THE INTERNET

There are many different kinds of resources available on the Internet, from the vastly popular World Wide Web to newsgroups, listservs, and gopher sites. While it would be impossible to even scratch the surface of the information available to you on the Internet, we hope to give you an idea of the scope of research tools to be found. If you are new to the Internet, we recommend that you purchase a comprehensive guide, such as *The Internet Complete Reference* by Harley Hahn and Rick Stout.

THE WORLD WIDE WEB

What is the World Wide Web? It is a part of the Internet on which people or companies can upload Web pages, or Web sites that may range in nature from educational to commercial. You are as likely to stumble onto a page about Tide detergent as you are to find information about tides around the world or the tides at the Bay of Fundy. The number of computers providing information on the Web currently doubles about every two months.

The Web has two features that make it especially attractive: hypertext and multimedia. Hypertext links mean you can move from one document to another simply by clicking on a highlighted word or set of words. For example, you may see a main menu that looks like this:

RESEARCH SMART
• Getting Started
• Indexes and Abstracts
• Electronic Databases
• The World Wide Web

By double-clicking on any of the underlined topics, you will go directly to information about that subject (no messy page turning!). You may also see a link to other Web sites. This allows you to find sources that are related to the page you are looking at. Hypertext links are created using Hypertext Markup Language or HTML. That is why documents on the Web may be referred to as HTML or Web documents. You may also see them referred to as Web pages or home pages.

WEB BROWSERS

So, the World Wide Web is out there, but you can't look at it unless you have access to a Web browser and an Internet Service Provider (ISP). Most universities offer their students access to the Internet with a college account. Netscape and Microsoft Explorer, are the more popular browsers. They allow you to view the pictures, films, and sounds you can access on the World Wide Web.

URLs

Now that you're hooked up, you still need to know how to get somewhere. URL stands for Uniform Resource Locator. It is the address of a document located on the Web. For example, if you wanted to look up the Web page for courses given by The Princeton Review, you would have to enter the URL http://www.review.com/courses into the correct spot on your Web browser.

What are all those components of the URL?

http:// is the part that shows that this is a World Wide Web document. If you saw gopher:// in front of a URL, you would be retrieving a gopher document.

www.review.com tells you the address of the main machine where the information is stored.

/courses is the path of the document. Once the browser connects with the review.com computer, it must follow a path to the /courses directory.

You may notice that the main names in the URL end with one of the following common suffixes: *.com* (indicating a commercial enterprise), *.edu* (an educational institution), or *.org* (an organization).

WEB SEARCH ENGINES

What if you don't know the URL for a document? You may not even know what you are looking for. Don't panic. You may use any of a number of search engines located on the World Wide Web to help you locate information in your subject area.

There are two main types of search vehicles: subject indexes and search engines. Though the distinction may not seem great, it is useful to distinguish the two in the name of good, efficient searching. You may be paying for Internet access time, and therefore do not want to waste valuable minutes doing useless searches.

A subject index is the best way to browse for sites if you have only a subject in mind. They allow you to get progressively selective by narrowing down your subject field through a search tree. For example, if you click on the general subject category *Arts* you will be presented with a dozen or so subcategories – such as *Museums, Art Review Grants* and *Artists*. Click on *Artists* and you will be presented again with a dozen or so different artists who have some sort of Web page. If you click on *Claude Monet*, you will find that there is the Claude Monet home page.

Click on that and your browser will send you to:

http://www.columbia.edu/~jns16/
monet_html/monet.html.

On the Claude Monet home page you will find information about Monet, from "An Introduction to Monet and his Art," to "A Discussion of Monet's Methods and Techniques," to "A Formal Analysis of one of Monet's Works." There is a bibliography of sources used to create the site and several images of Monet's paintings. There are also links to related sites. As you can see, the Claude Monet home page would be a very useful site for your research paper on Monet. You may also search by initiating a keyword search at any point along the narrowing-down process. You will usually be asked if you want the engine to search the whole database or only those sites in your narrowed-down subject.

The most popular subject indexes on the Web are:

Subject Index	URL	Notes
Yahoo!	http://www.yahoo.com	Yahoo! will search another database—AltaVista—if it doesn't locate anything for your search in Yahoo!
Excite	http://www.excite.com	You can browse handpicked "reviewed sites" on Excite's huge database
A2Z	http://a2z.lycos.com	
Magellan Internet Guide	http://www.mckinley.com	
Web Crawler Select	http://www.Webcrawler.com	
Galaxy	http://galaxy.einet.net/galaxy.html	
Infoseek Ultrasmart	http://www.infoseek.com	
The WWW Virtual Library	http://www.w3.org/vl/	Will arrange subjects by Library of Congress subject headings.

The other type of searching you can do is with a search engine. Here, you enter your keyword or keywords (most allow Boolean searches) and you will be given a list of sites that match your search terms. Most of these engines will rank the sites by how closely they match what you asked for. If you requested sites by searching "Theodore AND Roosevelt AND Police," the first things listed would be those that matched the most searched terms. There is usually a short description or possible review of the sites returned to you. You only need to click on a name to go straight to that site.

Some of the most popular search engines are:

Search Engine	URL	Notes
Lycos	http://www.lycos.com	
Web Crawler	http://Webcrawler.com	
Infoseek	http://www.infoseek.com	Infoseek's Ultraseek will search through a fast, huge database with Boolean logic, automatically searching on word variations and possible misspellings.
AltaVista	http://www.altavista.digital.com	AltaVista's Advanced Search uses Boolean logic and gives you options about how you would like results ranked.
Search.com	http://www.search.com	
Hot Bot	http://www.hotbot.com/index.html	

Whether you decide to search with a subject index or a search engine, you should always search at least two different databases. Because of the huge amount of information on the Internet, no one search tool could possibly contain all sites. You may strike out in one spot and strike gold in another. Have a few search strategies in mind as you begin.

OTHER INTERNET DIRECTORIES AND REFERENCE PAGES

There are some Web sites that are useful for students to know. You should check out your university's home page—many list resources that are helpful for research. If your school does not have an Internet site, check out the site for any large university. There are more resources than we can possibly list. Use the links at these sites to lead you to sites that may be even more useful.

In addition, most colleges have arrangements for their students to use online services that charge a fee—such as *Britannica Online*. Check into that by accessing your college's home page.

Internet Public Library
http://ipl.sils.umich.edu
One of the Internet's better attempts at a library without walls. There are links here to many resources by type or subject.

AltaVista
http://www.altavista.digital.com and
DejaNews
http://www.dejanews.com
These search engines allow you to search through full texts of Newsgroup postings.

Yahoo!'s Image Surfer
http://ipix.yahoo.com
Interpix Image Search Tool and Subject Directory
http://isurf.interpix.com
These engines allow you to search from images on the Internet by subject.

Bartlett's Quotations
http://www.columbia.edu/acis/bartleby/bartlett
Online version of the famous book allows you to search using keywords or by author. There is an alphabetical index of all authors and a chronological index of primary authors. The site is maintained by Columbia University's online editors.

Chiefs of State and Cabinet Ministers of Foreign Governments
http://www.odci.gov/cia/publications/chiefs/chiefs-toc-view.html
A comprehensive list of presidents, cabinet ministers, heads of central banks, ambassadors to the United States, and heads of state for most world governments. This site is maintained by the Central Intelligence Agency.

The World Factbook
http://www.odci.gov/cia/publication/95fact
Information from many government agencies about every country in the world. This information is updated annually. A great place to find out about the geography, people, government, economics, and communications of a country. A map appears on each page with the country information.

Population Index
http://popindex.princeton.edu
A site maintained by the Office of Population Research, Princeton University. The information is updated quarterly. Here you can access information about fertility and mortality rates, population size, growth, and historical demography from 1934 to the present for many countries.

The On-Line Books Page
http://www.cs.cmu.edu/books.html
An index to thousands of full text online books. This site only indexes those books that appear both full text and free of charge. You can search by author or title, browse by author, title or subject heading.

E-Journal
http://www.edoc.com/ejournal
An index to electronic journals on the Internet. It is maintained by the WWW Virtual Library. The site indexes academic and reviewed journals, college or university journals, e-mail newsletters, magazines, newspapers, political and print magazines, publishing topics, and business/finance journals. It also links to related Internet resources.

Biography
http://biography.com/find/find.html
This site, maintained by the Arts & Entertainment television network, enables users to access short biographical entries. You may search by name or browse alphabetically. Pages are cross-referenced and information sources are cited.

National Geographic Society's Map Machine Atlas
http://www.nationalgeographic.com/ngs/maps/atlas/index.html
You can find maps, flags, facts, and profiles of the countries of the world at this site maintained by the National Geographic Society.

Chemicool Periodic Table of the Elements
http://the-tech.mit.edu/chemical
You can search by entering an element name into the search field or by clicking directly on the elements spot on the full-color periodic table.

Greek Mythology
http://intergate.net/uhtml/.jhunt/greek_myth/greek_myth.html
On this page you can find information about the Greek and Roman gods, heroes, creatures, and stories of Greek mythology. There are also links to related Internet resources.

Hypertext Webster's Interface
http://c.gp.cs.cmu.edu:5103/prog/webster
Allows wild card searching so that you may look up a word without knowing exactly how to spell it. Also provides a correction list for a word you've misspelled.

Currency Exchange Rates
http://www.dna.lth.se/cgi-bin/kurt/rates
Choose the country whose rate interests you, then choose the rate you need to compare it to. Rates are updated frequently.

A FINAL WORD ON THE INTERNET

The amount of information at your fingertips makes the Internet a most appealing reference tool. A word of caution: One of the biggest problems with using Internet resources as references is their very nature. Pages may be updated, changed or deleted. Sites that sound official are not necessarily so. (The "Official Dan Rather Home Page" may have no "official" status, and may contain inaccurate information.)

There is no policing body on the Internet. Many claim this is its strength. It does behoove you as a researcher to carefully document your sources and look for sites affiliated with reputable institutions—universities, publishing houses, newspapers, and the like. An online version of a standard reference work is most likely reliable. *Britannica Online,* for example, is as reliable a source as the printed version.

We don't want to scare you away from a valuable resource—just use it with caution.

WRITING AN OUTLINE

Before you write an outline, make a list of the main questions you plan to answer and the important facts you have discovered as you've gone through your sources. For example, if you're doing a paper on the composer Mozart and his rival Salieri, you may come up with a list that looks like this:

- Background history of Mozart

- Salieri's background

- Mozart's development as a composer

- Mozart had a lot of ups and downs

- Salieri was quite jealous

- Mozart's mysterious death

Now that you have most of your sources ready, you can write a preliminary outline. This is a good time to give serious thought to how you plan to organize your paper. There are some basic ways to go about it:

Chronological Order

This is the most straightforward way to organize the information in your paper—simply in the order in which it happened. If you were telling the story of your paper and found yourself using words like *first, second, then,* and *next,* you probably have information that is best written about in chronological order. Histories and biographical information work best when presented this way.

Cause and Effect

Your paper will be written to show that one thing was the cause, the next was the effect. This is similar to a chronological form. For example, show that there was an increase in violence on television, then, as a result, there was an increase in violent behavior in children. Use this format to prove your thesis that there is a correlation between violence on television and violent behavior.

Spatial Order

This works best for more narrative papers: You tell the story as it might have been seen. You may describe a situation as it looks from a distance (group attacking a man) and then show how the story changes as you get closer (the group is actually helping the man). Use this highly visual style to make a point and keep a narrative lively, or to describe a scene.

Order of Importance

Here, you make your most important point first, and move to points that are not as meaningful. You may also order the paper in a reverse order of importance—begin with the least important points and move to the most significant ones.

Categorical Order

Some topics naturally fall into categories. If you were writing a paper examining different medical procedures, you would want to divide the different sections into each procedure you plan to examine.

Opposition Order

This is a sort of point–counterpoint-style paper. If you have two or more points of view, you may want to present them this way: The first section dealing with the one point of view, the next with the other, the following with how they are the same, then a final section that tells how they differ.

Obviously, the subject of your paper will help you decide how you want to present your information. You may combine styles as well. Your primary goal is to get across information in the clearest method possible. Once you decide on the best way to organize your information, you are ready to write the outline for your paper.

Many computer programs will write an outline for you, but here is its basic format:

I.
   A.
   B.
      1.
      2.
         (a)
         (b)

II.
   A.
      1.
      2.
   B.
      1.
      2.
         (a)
         (b)
            (1.)
            (2.)

You should make as many divisions as you feel are necessary. The Roman numerals represent the major divisions of the paper. The subdivisions represent smaller categories within the major divisions. In general, if you're going to subdivide a topic, you should have at least two divisions. You want your outline to be detailed, to the appropriate extent. You're looking to keep your paper and your thoughts organized. The outline comes relatively early in the process; if you have too much detail, it will be harder to be flexible with your ideas.

We highly recommend writing your outline on a computer word processing program, if possible. It will be much easier to amend your document as necessary.

Here is a sample outline for our Mozart paper:

I. Mozart's life
  A. Early childhood—he was a prodigy at age four
  B. Success as a young man
  C. Meeting people at the court

II. Salieri's Life
  A. Moderate success
  B. Bitter towards many rivals

III. The plot thickens
  A. Mozart and Salieri meet
    1. Mozart is brash and brilliant
    2. Salieri is refined yet limited
    3. Mozart gets more recognition
  B. Mozart writes his great symphonies
    1. They get only moderate attention
    2. Mozart panics
    3. Becomes a Freemason
  C. Mozart's letters to his fellow masons
    1. Reflect his unhappiness
    2. Talks about his fears
      (a) about life
      (b) about his family
      (c) about his talent

IV. Mozart's death

    A. He had just finished three operas

    B. Never saw financial reward

        1. Who was responsible?

        2. No one there to help his wife, Constanze

    C. Died a pauper—buried in a pauper's grave

        1. The plague

        2. Murder?

            (a) suspect #1—Salieri

            (b) other possible suspects

    D. Conclusion: Mozart was murdered

You will use your headings and subheadings to guide you through the note-taking process. You may want to reference the part of the outline you're taking notes for on your note card. For example, you may use the subheading "He had just finished three operas" or the corresponding outline numbers, IV A, to reference a note card that contains information about that part of your paper.

NOTE CARDS

Now that you are beginning to find information that looks as if it may be of interest to you, you should start to compile what is called a *working bibliography*. Why working? Because you want to be flexible at these early stages of research about what you will eventually use to write your paper. There are two ways to compile a working bibliography: with note cards or on a computer file of some sort.

The traditional way is to record your bibliographic information on note cards, using one note card for each source. The great advantage to working this way (as opposed to recording all your information on one sheet of paper) is that you can easily discard and add sources, and when the time comes, you can arrange them in the proper order so that you can make a bibliography.

The other way is to use the computer to generate a database.

Your options are to:

- Use the table function on your word processing program. This allows you to create fields for each important piece of information you need to store. Many programs will automatically alphabetize your list when you're done.

- Use an Excel spreadsheet. Again, you can organize all the pieces of information into different fields.

- Use a notecard type program that allows you to type up the bibliographic information for each source on a separate "card" that files it away.

- Simply use your word processing program and edit your list as needed.

Use the method you feel most comfortable with. Despite the allure of technology, many people still like to use the traditional note cards because they are more easily transported and can be filled out while you examine the material.

What Should I Write on a Note Card?

No matter how you decide to compile your information, what you need to record will remain the same. You should always include:

- Title of the book, article, or journal

- The full name of the author, editor(s), translator(s), etc.

- The full name of the publisher and where the work was published.

- The date of publication.

- The pages you are referencing.

You can imagine how annoying it is to record incomplete bibliographic information, only to have to find the source again when you are writing a final bibliography. A little extra work at this stage of the game will save you countless hours of backtracking later on.

Try to keep your format consistent, so that you will always know you've gotten all the information you need. We recommend highly that you note the call numbers or the location of the reference in case you need to find it again. Just jot it in the upper right-hand corner of the card, or as a column in your database.

FOR A BOOK

1. Author's name (Last name, First name, Middle initial).
2. Full title of the book, including any subtitles.
3. Editor or translator if one exists.
4. Edition.
5. If the book is a multivolume set, the number of the volume you are using and the number of volumes in the whole set.
6. If the book is part of a series, the series name.
7. City of publication.
8. Publisher.
9. Year of publication.

Sample book note card

(Numbers in parentheses refer to numbers above.)

```
(1)  Jones, Alice C.                    (CALL NUMBER) MS
(2)  Theories on Mozart's Death                      495
(3)  Relish, Petra R. translator                     M5
(4)  2nd edition                                     J48
(5)  volume 7 of 30
(6)  Great Composers Series
(7)  Prague
(8)  Morbid Press
(9)  1995
```

Sample table entry

Author	Jones, Alice C.
Title	Theories on Mozart's Death
Editor/Translator	Relish, Petra R, translator
Edition	2nd edition
Volume #	7 of 30
Series	Great Composers Series
City of Pub	Prague
Publisher	Morbid Press
Year of Pub	1995
Call #	MS 495 M5 J48

For a Journal

1. Author's name
2. Title of the article
3. Title of the journal
4. Volume number and issue number
5. Year of publication
6. Page numbers of the article

Sample journal note card

(1) Richly, Ari

(2) "Mozart and His Death: Mystery of the Ages"

(3) Composer's Quarterly

(4) v. 3, issue 8

(5) 1997

(6) 111-118

Sample journal database

Author	Richly, Ari
Title	(1) "Mozart and His Death: Mystery of the Ages"
Journal	Composer's Quarterly
Volume/Issue	v. 3, issue 8
Year of Pub.	1997
Page #s	111-118

FOR A MAGAZINE OR NEWSPAPER

1. Author's full name
2. Title of article
3. Title of periodical
4. Date of publication
5. Pages of the article

Sample newspaper article note card

(1) Fullman, James M.

(2) "Mozart: New Theories on an Old Death?"

(3) Sun City Times

(4) May 15, 1995

(5) p. 45-46

Sample newspaper article database

Author	Fullman, James M.
Title	"Mozart: New Theories on an Old Death?"
Magazine or Paper	Sun City Times
Date of publication	May 15, 1995
Pages	p. 45-46

Many professors will want a copy of your working bibliography early on in your research to be sure that you are on the right track. If you've maintained a list or database on your computer, you can simply print it out.

This is all of the information you will need to prepare your final bibliography. There are several programs available for preparing the final bibliography. We will discuss them later in the bibliography format section.

TAKING NOTES

It seems that everyone has his or her favorite way to take notes. Naturally, note cards are extremely useful here as well. If your working bibliography is recorded on note cards, then you can keep all the note cards on a source together with its bibliographic card. In any case, you should have some code or system that will identify the source of the note card.

You don't have to use note cards, however. Some students like to write out their notes on sheets of paper; some like to keep them all in a notebook. Remember, whatever your method, a little careful work now will save you a lot of trouble in the final stages of writing.

Some rules for note-taking:

1. Keep notes for different sources on different sheets of paper or different sets of note cards.

2. Clearly label notes taken from the same source. You may want to:

    Number each source document and write that number on the top of the page or note card.

    or

    Write the author's name at the top of each page or card.

3. Keep note-taking to a minimum.

What do we mean by that last statement? It is a great temptation to take too many notes. You are then faced with a plethora of information that you need to whittle down. Trust yourself as you go through your sources. Most students take too many notes because they are worried that there's some small detail that they may need later on, even if it doesn't seem important now. Of course, if you're really not sure, it is easier to throw out a note card than to look for a piece of information again at the eleventh hour.

There are three types of information you will take for notes:

- A summary of the facts you've learned, culled into a few sentences or a short paragraph.

- A paraphrase of the information you've read. In this case, you aren't really leaving out too much—just putting a section of the author's work in your own words.

- A quotation from the literature. Sometimes you come across a piece of information that is perfect not just for what it says, but for the way it is said. In this case, you want to quote directly. Always put quotation marks around a note you've quoted directly. It is very important to remember that these are not your words, and to give credit where credit is due.

In all these cases, you must be careful to record exactly where you got the information you've taken notes for. You're going to need all those page numbers for footnotes (Ack! Footnotes!). Just write the page number up in the corner of your card, or right next to the note entry in your notebook.

Keep entries short. A rule of thumb is that you should have one "idea" per note. That probably means about a sentence or two. Maybe three.

Sample Note Card

```
Source 1.                                                    p. 45
     Finished The Magic Flute (Die Zauberflote) 1791—never enjoyed the
     financial reward.
```

How many note cards should you take? How many notes do you need to have? Naturally, this will depend greatly on the length and type of your project.

THE THESIS STATEMENT

You may be called upon to present a thesis statement. The thesis statement is just that—a statement. It is not a question. You can, however, use a question to form a thesis statement. All you need to do is answer it. For example, if your preliminary research has led you to wonder: "Was Mozart poisoned by his rival, Salieri?" All you need to do to turn this into a thesis statement is to answer the question the way you *suspect* your research will go. For example, your thesis statement may be that:

> "Mozart was not poisoned by Salieri, but rather died of the plague, a common affliction of the time."

> or

> "Mozart was poisoned by his jealous rival, Salieri, in one of the great murders of the day."

You may want to present a statement that has some background information in it, explaining just a line or two about your thesis, for example:

"Mozart was one of the great composers of all time. Despite the great amount we know about his life, his death has always been shrouded in mystery. It is my intention to show that Mozart was in fact poisoned by his jealous rival, Salieri, in one of the great unpunished murders of all time."

You don't need to know ahead of time what the answer will be. It is, however, appropriate to do some research before you pose your thesis. You don't want a situation in which you have no answer. You want to be certain that there is enough scholarly work on the subject for you to draw some sort of conclusion. Although it is possible to reach a conclusion that one can't tell how Mozart died, obviously it is preferable, and more satisfying, to either prove or disprove your thesis.

Most professors will want your thesis statement before you get too far along in a project so that they may help you if your scope is too broad or your topic is too unfocused. You may also modify your thesis statement as you proceed. You may find that your thesis is a little off and further clarification is necessary. Perhaps you discover that it wasn't Salieri, but another composer of the time who is most suspect in Mozart's mysterious death.

A good thesis statement will give direction to your research. It is a goal you set out to attain, and prevents you from becoming diverted.

TIP

Print out a copy of your thesis statement and tape it up next to your desk. Always remember what you are looking to prove or disprove.

CHAPTER 2

The First Draft

Let's review some of the steps you should have completed by this time:

1. You've narrowed down your topic and conducted preliminary research. You need to have a clear vision of your topic.

2. You've done a thorough search of the library reference sources and other outside sources (such as the Internet). At this stage, you should know exactly which sources you are going to use for your research.

3. You've written the thesis statement. This will help keep you focused on the purpose of your research.

4. You've written a preliminary outline. An outline will give structure and organization to your writing.

5. You've got a working bibliography. This will enable you to cite your sources properly and give credit with citations and bibliography.

6. You've read and taken notes from your sources. You can't write about a subject with authority until you've completed all the reading.

If you've completed all these steps, you are ready to write the rough draft. The first step in writing is to get all your information together and organize it properly. Get out your note cards, outline, and a good dictionary.

You will need to separate your note cards into piles. Use your outline as a guide. You should put all the cards dealing with each section on your outline together. This is a good time to assess the order of the topics you will discuss. You may choose to rearrange some of the information. Don't think that it is a waste of your time to rewrite your outline. If your vision has changed, so should your outline. By the time your research is at this stage, you should have a better grasp on your subject matter than you did when you first began.

If you don't have a computer with a word-processing program, it's a good idea to find out how you can gain access to one. Most universities make computers available to their students. The process of writing any paper of more than two or three pages will be greatly facilitated by the use of a word-processing program.

Before you set pen to paper (or fingers to keyboard), it may be very helpful for you to discuss your ideas with a classmate or advisor. After you've done the reading and written your outline, talking to someone will help get your creative juices flowing. It may also help you to determine if you need to do any additional last-minute work.

Everyone has a different style for writing the first draft of a paper. Some people are such perfectionists that they write the first draft slowly and methodically, producing a document that needs very little revision. We recommend writing a little more quickly than that. The first draft should be just that: A document that will need at least some revision. For many writers, getting all the information down on paper is the hardest part. Going back and revising will not be nearly as difficult. So, don't worry too much about how well you are writing the first draft. It's much easier to decide what work remains to be done once you have written a full first draft.

What should be included in the first draft? We recommend leaving out any direct quotations and writing as much as you can without referring too much to your notes. Overemphasis on your notes may lead to a good deal of unintentional paraphrasing and a lack of originality. Write as much as you can, using your note cards as a guide, and punch up your paper with facts and quotations on the rewrite.

THE TITLE

You don't need a title at this stage of the writing process. It may help you, however, to have a working title. Again, each student has his own method. Some like to write the title first, and others last, after all the work has been completed.

Your title should give the reader an idea of the scope of your paper. You may want it to be a little witty or creative. You may prefer a more dignified, academic title. Let your subject matter guide you. If the paper is more casual than formal, and your instructor encourages creativity, have fun. Here are a few examples of titles for a paper on tenement reform in New York City.

1. The straightforward title: Jacob Riis and Tenement Reform in New York City at the Turn of the Century.

2. Use a date and colon: Jacob Riis and Tenement Reform: New York, 1912–1920.

3. Use a subtitle: Tenement Reform in New York City: Legislating Social Change in the Twentieth Century.

4. Use a "headline" for a more creative slant: Slum No More: Jacob Riis Brings Real Changes to Tenements.

These are just suggestions. Naturally, you will have your own style when it comes to writing the title. If you are hesitant, use a simple working title and alter it as you go along. We will review the information needed for the title page in the next chapter.

THE ABSTRACT

Some professors want an abstract written at the beginning of the paper, particularly if you are writing a thesis. The abstract is a brief summary of your paper. It should state the goals and the results of your research. It may run from a paragraph to a half a page in length. A sample of an abstract is:

An Analysis of Tenement Reform in New York City at the Turn of Century

The purpose of this study was to research the effects of the Tenement Law of 1901—the "new law"—on the quality of life for the residents of tenements in New York City. The study contrasts this new law with the Tenement Law of 1869, or "old law." The works of Jacob Riis and Ernest Flagg, in addition to several prominent charity organizations, are examined as well. Articles written at the time, photographs of tenements, and immigrant stories are all examined. I conclude that there were significant changes in the quality of life as a result of these laws, which themselves were a result of a new idea of human life and its value.

The information uncovered indicates that the changes were indeed far-reaching, past the tenements and into the lives of all New Yorkers, and that the reason so much changed was not just a renewed sense of humanity, but a change in the outlook of citizens in general.

THE PARTS OF THE PAPER—AN OVERVIEW

While your outline should guide your general format, there are certain criteria that must be included in every paper.

BEGINNINGS

You set the tone for your whole paper in the introduction. Don't be coy when you start writing. State your thesis or goal and how you intend to answer any questions raised by the assignment. Anyone reading the introduction should have a clear vision of the content of your research paper.

The purpose of the introduction is to give a clear statement of intent and process. If you worry about trying to impress your teachers with flowery language or great length, you will fail. Put yourself in your teacher's place. She has to read dozens of papers and will be happiest with those that are clear, well-written, and do exactly what they set out to do: prove a thesis, or demonstrate comprehension. If you force humor or erudition, it will sound that way. Let your style evolve naturally as you write. Your first big research papers will not be as good as the ones you write later. Just concentrate on writing a competent, well-documented paper, not a literary masterpiece.

Consider your audience when you write the paper. Is the paper meant to be formal or casual? Are you addressing your peers or just your instructor? Is your paper meant to be factual and dispassionate, or are you taking a side, pleading a cause? There's no right or wrong answer to these questions. You just need to contemplate how you want to present the paper. In the absence of any specific instructions, it is always safe to assume that you are writing for someone who is intelligent and knowledgeable, but not necessarily familiar with the specifics of your topic. This will ensure that you write a paper that clearly outlines your research without talking down to the reader.

Although some teachers frown on overuse of the word *I* in a paper, it does have its place in the introduction and conclusion. If your teacher is dead-set against *I*, you may use a phrase like "this paper will show...". Here are some examples of opening sentences for different research papers.

> Nietzsche was one of the most controversial philosophers of his time, and his controversy has not diminished over the years. While his major works had many brilliant insights, it is my intention to prove that Nietzsche's concept of the *uberman* or *superman* was a direct influence on Hitler's philosophy of the Aryan race.

Do you have an interesting fact on hand? Start off you paper with that:

> While it is easy to dismiss the effects of advertising, consider this: While only a small percentage of adult smokers smoke Camel cigarettes, almost 85 percent of children (under

the age of sixteen) who smoke, smoke Camels. I will show that the "Joe Camel" campaign, far from a fun, silly advertisement, is in fact a blatant attempt to capture young children and get them hooked on cigarettes.

Another sample:

The scope of the modern public library has gone far beyond that of a "loaner of books." While books still form its foundation, the modern library has begun to collect videos, computer equipment, children's games, and more. One library in a rural community was even known to loan out farm equipment. Is the modern library in danger of becoming so diffuse as to lose its vision and primary purpose? What does it mean to keep up with the times? The purpose of this paper is to prove that the modern public library is in desperate need of a mission statement that encompasses more than just lending books, or it shall become nothing more than an unused decrepit museum.

You may want to set the scene if you are doing historical research, such as the type we gave for an abstract earlier.

The twentieth century was approaching in New York City, and the 1869 tenement law, now dubbed the "old law," was being called to question. People like Jacob Riis and the architect Ernest Flagg sought the reform that would bring light and air into the homes of the poor. Charity organizations around New York City fought for this cause as well, and soon the changes were embodied in the Tenement Law of 1901—the "new law." These "new law" tenements largely embodied the plans of Ernest Flagg. The new design allowed for a more humane environment without sacrificing efficiency. The courtyard style tenement was born. In what follows, I will show that the effects of this reform were far-reaching and their causes were surprising.

Let's review what these introductory paragraphs have that make them satisfactory introductions.

1. A clear statement of purpose. Whether you say specifically "I plan to prove..." or "The purpose of this paper is to..." just make sure that your reader knows what you're writing about within the first few paragraphs.

2. A little background information. It's usually a good idea to give your reader at least a few sentences about the background of your topic. While you will most certainly elaborate on ideas you are just setting out in your introduction, you need to give some sort of lead-in. Do you have an interesting quotation or statistic? These can be excellent ways to introduce a subject.

3. A few questions. This can be an effective way to introduce your thesis. Ask questions you suspect your reader may have. Assure him that you will be addressing these questions by posing them yourself. Don't, however, ask simple questions and answer them. For example: "What is a tenement? Most consider any low-income housing unit to be a tenement" is weak. If you don't think your reader knows what a tenement is, inform him.

4. A positive view of the end point of your paper. You should know by now exactly what your thesis statement is. You may have fiddled with your orignal idea for a thesis so that your research supports it. Don't mess around with statements like "I hope to prove..." "The facts may show..." or "It is possible that..." Be bold. Say "I will prove..." "The facts will show..." or "It is clear that..." This doesn't sound like bragging—it proves to your reader that you are a confident writer.

5. A positive view of the topic itself. Don't ever start off by apologizing for your topic, research or ideas. If you don't feel good about what you are writing, you will end up with a less than satisfactory paper. Don't say something like "Though there was not much information on this topic..." or "While the assertions I will make may sound foolish..." You don't want your reader to start off by looking for flaws in your writing. If your topic wasn't a good one, or the information was scarce, you should have moved to a different topic, right?

How long should the introduction be? Naturally, that depends on the length of your paper, but we believe that most introductions can be satisfactorily accomplished in as little as a paragraph to as much as a page. Don't waste too much of your reader's time telling her what you will say and will do—say it and do it!

REVIEW OF THE LITERATURE

As you get past the beginning, into the meat of the paper, it is necessary to present the facts for your case. You need to prove that you have completed the research part of the research paper and that you've comprehended what you've read and its relevance to your subject. You want to show respect for the scholars whose work you have read and prove your own authority in the meantime. How will you present the different sources you have consulted? Refer to your outline. Remember that whether you are presenting chronologically or in order of importance, your sources must be considered. Here are a few things to think about as you analyze each one:

1. Describe the source. You will be citing it, of course, but beyond the bibliographic description, you need to give your reader some information about the authority and content of what you have chosen to use. For example: "Hampshire's discussion of predicting and deciding resonates through many of his previous works, and has generated quite a lot of discussion in the field."

   or

   "The text is illustrated with pictures of the illuminated manuscripts to which the author refers."

   While it is not necessary to give biographic information on each author, or the publishing history of every book, it is helpful to give some background information, especially if your reader may not be familiar with the source material. You usually need to summarize the content to some degree. Don't assume complete familiarity with your source material.

2. Analyze the work. Do you agree or disagree with the author's thesis? While you don't need to attack the conclusions the author makes, you may be able to attack some of the premises. You don't want to simply agree with every author you present. It is good to show that you are using a skeptical eye as you read. That doesn't mean, however, that you should trash each of your sources one by one. For the most part, you choose works that you respect and cite sources that will support your central thesis or goal.

3 Credit the source. Don't forget to give credit to the ideas you are describing and analyzing.

The body of the paper should be constructed of sections similar to this. You are slowly building the foundation of the pyramid—leading to one central point at the top. If your base is not sturdy enough, your point will not be made. Follow your outline. Keep your thoughts organized. Refer to the style guide in the next chapter to familiarize yourself with some of the basics of grammar and citation. While this is a rough draft, that doesn't mean it should be as sloppy as possible. The clearer your presentation at this point, the better your final product will be.

KEEP IT MOVING

Be aware of how your paper is moving along. Does it jump from topic to topic, or have an interesting flow? Can your reader follow your train of thought? Keep in mind that paragraphs are the building blocks of any paper. They will help to keep your ideas separate and clear. You need to be aware of how you move from one sentence to the next within a paragraph and from one paragraph to the next. There are several methods to help you move through your paper seamlessly.

A paragraph should represent a coherent idea. Although it is not necessary, beginning writers (and those writing first drafts) should start each paragraph with a topic sentence, and use the rest of the paragraph to expound upon that sentence. For example, let's take the sentence:

> The crime mystery novel took shape in the nineteenth century in France, England, and the United States.

Use the rest of the paragraph to *explain* what you mean by that:

> This new genre was enormously popular in these countries, where many different writers took advantage of the emergence of an organized police force and the public's lurid interest in crime to sell books and engage readers. Topics that had previously been considered "impolite" were among the most popular of the nineteenth century.

This represents a unified thought. Paragraphs can relate to each other in many ways. Look at the myriad ways we can introduce the next paragraph in this paper to see how one paragraph may relate to another.

1. Contrast the point you just made. Consider using contrasting words, like *however*, *but*, or *nevertheless*.

   However, murder mysteries have a more important function than lurid interest.

2. Give specific examples. Use phrases like *for example, such as* or *illustrated by* to introduce your examples

   For example, Edgar Allan Poe's "Murders in the Rue Morgue" was considered to be the first crime mystery.

3. Give the cause(s) of your previous paragraph. "The reasons for..." "Because..." "Therefore..." and "Consequently..." are all good ways to introduce causes.

   The reasons for the interest in this new genre were numerous.

4. Give the effects of your previous paragraph.

   The effects of such popularity were far-reaching. Move chronologically to the next idea. "Later..." "Subsequent to..." or "Since that time..." are all good transitional statements.

   Since its emergence in the nineteenth century, the genre has become even more popular.

5. Give more information about your previous paragraph. Consider phrases like "In addition..." "Furthermore..." or "Finally..."

   Furthermore, the emergence of a strongly organized police force in these countries...

Refer again to your outline. See the general pattern for how you intend to tell your story and unfold your research. Rely on the simple phrases above to carry you from one sentence to the next, from one paragraph to another. These simple structural points will help your reader to follow your points more easily. While you should be careful not to overuse these phrases, you can edit them in your final draft.

ARE YOU STUCK?

There will come a point in your writing when you will become stuck. It happens to everyone. That doesn't mean that you're not prepared to write your paper. If you have done all your research properly, it will come. Here are a few tips to get you out of your writing slump.

1. Review your class notes. Was there some question raised in class that might shed light on your current dilemma?

2. Evaluate your structure. Would it be easier to present your sources chronologically, rather than, say, in order of importance? Sometimes looking at a problem from a different angle makes it easier to solve.

3. Reread the assignment or your thesis statement. Have you lost sight of your goals? Some writers get so wrapped up in the writing process, they forget what they are writing about.

4. Read what you have written so far. How does it sound? Is there something missing?

5. Talk to a classmate or advisor about the assignment. Talking through a problem can be very enlightening.

6. Just write. Sometimes forcing yourself to finish can be the best way to work through a block. Don't forget that this is a rough draft—you will have time to revise later. Many writers hit blocks simply by worrying needlessly about how every word sounds.

Conclusions

Now that you have gone though all your material, describing and critiquing it, you are ready to start making conclusions. It is usually a good idea at this point (especially if your paper is more than a few pages long) to summarize what you have already said. By this we mean a paragraph or two that simply states what your process was in leading you up to this point. For example:

> "While Mozart's biographers have covered aspects of his life from the purely factual to the sensational, all have raised similar suspicions. As we have seen, his death has been described in a variety of ways, but always as mysterious. We have also seen, through the various accounts of Mozart's life, Mozart himself was always controversial."

The conclusion should tie your paper together. Reread your introduction. You may want to make reference to statements made there as you are trying to wind up. Reread the review of the literature and make sure you are prepared to answer any and all questions you have raised in your paper.

Don't make grand statements about life that may sound wonderful, but are not supported by the information you have given. The single most important rule about the conclusion is that it must be supported. No new information should be introduced at this point. In fact, if you have done your job properly, the statements you make in your conclusion should be obvious, not startling, to your reader. Avoid using pat phrases like *In conclusion* and then simply restating your thesis. Your readers expect a little more than this.

Editing And Revising

Once you have a pretty complete version of your paper, you are ready to edit and revise. This is the stage at which you want to start adding direct quotations and organizing your citations and ideas. Once again, we cannot overstate the importance of rereading your work at each stage of the game. This is also the most dangerous time for a researcher, as you may be in danger of plagiarism. We will discuss in the next chapters all the finer points of grammar and form, but here are some general tips to start you cleaning up your paper.

1. Make sure you haven't overused phrases. Beginning writers tend to rely on certain phrases and use them way too often. Do you say things like *And therefore we can see* ... or *That is why* ... or some of the transitional and concluding phrases too much? Try to reword some of those sentences. If your paper is about Mozart, for example, do you start every other sentence with *Mozart*? Watch out, or you will sound repetitive.

2. Make sure the lengths of your sentences and paragraphs vary. If every sentence is equal in length and all you paragraphs are four sentences, your paper will look and sound boring. Alternating longer sentences with shorter ones and punching several short paragraphs between longer ones will keep your reader interested.

PLAGIARISM

Plagiarizing—whether intentional or not—is considered a serious offense. There are two possible reasons why students might plagiarize:

1. They honestly believe that no one will know they didn't come up with the material on their own. Keep in mind that your professors are extremely well-read in a variety of academic journals. While it may seem improbable to you that "anyone really reads this stuff," let us assure you that people do—the kind of people who are grading your papers. Teachers are trained to recognize a passage that stylistically doesn't match the rest of your paper. If you lift something and plunk it into the middle of your own writing, chances are good that it will stick out like a sore thumb.

2. They don't realize that they are plagiarizing. This is probably the more common
   reason for plagiarism. We like to think
   that if we didn't mean to do something, it
   isn't so bad; unfortunately, most schools
   won't take into account what your intentions were. While we summarize the rules
   for what you must cite, use this as a
   general guideline: If in doubt—cite!!!

How NOT to Plagiarize

What is plagiarism, exactly? Teachers have been wagging their
collective finger at students for years warning them of the horrors
that befall those who plagiarize. In fact, most universities take
plagiarism very seriously—some threaten expulsion for a student
who's been caught plagiarizing. Unfortunately, many students are
not really sure when they have crossed the line into plagiarism.

Plagiarism, n.

*the unauthorized use or close imitation of the language and
thoughts of another author and the representation of them
as one's own original work; something used and repre-
sented in this manner.*
from The Random House Unabridged Dictionary

As you can see, you don't necessarily have to copy someone's
work to plagiarize. You may be paraphrasing. If you do not give
some citation or credit to the author of the original work from
which you got a certain idea, table, drawing, or data, then you
have plagiarized. You must be very exact as you go through
your sources and begin the process of writing a research paper.
Citations, footnotes, and bibliography are important tools that
demonstrate to your professors and to your peers that you have
given credit where credit is due.

Some Useful Guidelines to Follow

- You must give credit to:

    Any direct quotation.

    Any indirect or paraphrased ideas from
    other sources.

A sequence of ideas or information; for example, a table or an interesting presentation of a topic.

Any opinion, theory or judgment formulated in one of your sources.

- You *don't* need to give credit to:

    Facts. This means that you don't need to document a fact that "everybody would know." Anything that can be looked up in a standard reference book is free for the taking. For example, you wouldn't need to give a reference for the scientific name of an animal.

    Old sayings, well-known Biblical scriptures, or familiar quotations such as *a cat has nine lives* would not need a citation.

- You may use your own material again. If, however, you are going to try to use the exact same paper for more than one course, you should probably check your school's policy.

- You may not hand in other students' papers and claim them as your own.

- When you take notes, use a special method to distinguish your own ideas from your source's ideas. You may use a different color pen, or bracket your own ideas.

- You must put quotation marks around a quote, even if it is one or two words long. If you are going to paraphrase, make sure you paraphrase from the earliest drafts of your paper. If you copy something directly with the idea that you'll paraphrase it later, you may forget and inadvertently plagiarize.

- Don't become intimidated when you are reading source material. Your teachers don't expect you to have the polished style of a published author. They will probably be more suspicious than impressed if you hand in a perfect-sounding paper that isn't your own. You are expected to sound like a student.

- When in doubt—cite. It is better to give credit for something that you didn't need to credit than to take credit for something you had no right to.

- Once you get in the habit of writing research papers, you will become more sophisticated about when and where to cite sources. At first, you may feel as though you are citing too much, but that's probably okay. We'll talk more in later chapters about developing your own ideas. Although a research paper relies on outside sources, always remember that it is your own voice that will distinguish it. Your professors are not looking for a string of quotes and rehashed ideas.

TIP

Try writing a first draft without using any of your notes. Naturally, it will be substantially shorter than the final draft. It will however, help you to keep your paper in your head—uncluttered by the quotes and citations that may bog you down. Then, you can go through and write a more thorough draft by adding all your source material.

3

Style Guide

It is most true, stilus virum arguit—our style betrays us.

—*Robert Burton*

STYLE GUIDE

When you start to write your paper, keep in mind that all the research in the world won't make up for bad writing. What is good writing? Good writing is precise, clear, and straightforward. Don't confuse using a lot of big words with sophisticated research. You can write a perfectly good paper that's readable by an average audience.

A QUICK AND PAINLESS GRAMMAR REVIEW

THE PARTS OF SPEECH

While we will not teach you English grammar from A to Z, it won't hurt to review the basics.

Noun: a person, place, thing or state of being
examples: Julie, girl, house, fence, truth, contentment, library

> The **girl** ran throughout the **streets** on the **day** of the **fair**.

Verb: the action in the sentence—a real action or a state of being
examples: run, jump, is, were, sing, play

> May **was** in the store on Saturday.

Adjective: describes a noun
examples: beautiful, silly, funny, wonderful, perfect, abrupt, ugly

> My **red** quilt is quite **beautiful**.

Adverb: describes a verb, an adjective or another adverb
examples: slowly, strangely, very, really, oddly, extremely

> Joe walked **very slowly** through the crowd.

Pronoun: replaces a noun
examples: he, she, they, it, we, me, you

> **He** wanted to be sure to find **her** in the store.

Preposition: places a noun
examples: in, out, around, through, within, about

> We went **to** the fair, **through** the line, **around** the Ferris wheel.

Interjection: used for emphasis
examples: wow! no! really!

> **Wow!** We won't have to take that test. **Yippee!**

Parts of the Sentence

Subject and Predicate

These parts of speech are used to make up sentences. There are two main parts of any sentence—the subject and the predicate. The subject is the main noun, the noun that is performing whatever action is happening in the sentence.

The predicate is just the rest of the sentence. The verb will be in the predicate. While the subject is often the first part of the sentence, it doesn't need to be. For example:

<table>
<tr><td style="text-align:center">Mary
subject</td><td style="text-align:center">went to Henry's for lunch.
predicate</td></tr>
<tr><td style="text-align:center">Mary's favorite place was
predicate</td><td style="text-align:center">the museum.
subject</td></tr>
</table>

If you are unsure about the subject, just locate the verb and ask yourself who or what performed it. For example, if you locate the verb *was* in the second example and ask yourself *what was?* the answer would be *the museum.*

Clauses and Phrases

A clause or a phrase is just a group of words that works as one in a sentence. That means you may have a whole group of words that describe the noun, instead of just one. That group of words acts as an adjective. For example:

Because the house was *on the lake*, it was quite beautiful.

The phrase *on the lake* describes the house, so it is an adverbial phrase. If the group of words has a subject and a verb, it is a clause, not a phrase. Here's an example:

Peanut butter, *which is a staple for many preschoolers*, is actually quite nutritious.

The group of words *which is a staple for many preschoolers*, is a clause—it has a subject (which) and a verb (is)—that acts as an adverb, describing peanut butter.

You don't need to know all the details about the differences between independent and dependent clauses, for example, or participial versus prepositional phrases. We just want you to be familiar with the terms, so that you'll understand them as we talk about finer points of style.

Voice

There are two kinds of voice you need to recognize: active and passive. The active voice is present whenever the subject of the sentence performs the action. For example:

<u>Mary</u>   <u>lost her library card.</u>
subject   predicate

In the passive voice, the subject receives the action. For example:

<u>The library card</u>   <u>was lost by Mary.</u>
subject   predicate

While it is very easy to slip into a passive voice when writing academic papers, it is always preferable to write in the active voice when possible. Compare the two examples:

> **Passive voice:** *The Magic Flute* was written by Mozart in 1791. Praise was heaped upon it by the court. However, fame made Mozart's contemporaries jealous. The opera was performed by opera companies all over Europe. Unfortunately, wealth was never enjoyed by Mozart.

> **Active voice:** Mozart wrote *The Magic Flute* in 1791. The court heaped great praise upon it. However, Mozart's contemporaries were jealous of his fame. Opera companies all over Europe performed the opera. Unfortunately, Mozart never enjoyed the wealth.

The active voice is much clearer. Why? It is immediately apparent to the reader who or what is performing the action in the sentence. The active voice is generally more concise. Wordiness is not a sign of erudition, only wordiness. The active voice makes for more interesting and even dramatic reading. The passive voice generally sounds stilted and odd.

This is not to say you should never use the passive voice. There are times when the performer of the action is unclear or unnecessary:

> The test was administered on a Saturday afternoon.

Some scientific writing employs the passive voice:

> The control group was used to verify the experiment.

FOUR IMPORTANT RULES YOU NEED TO KNOW.

1. Make sure that subject and verb agree. If your subject is plural, your verb needs to be plural. If your subject is singular, your verb needs to be singular. Don't be misled by confusing phrases that separate your subject and verb:

One of the boys **is** going to the store.

not

One of the boys **are** going to the store.

The subject is *one*, not *boys*

A few rules to help you avoid mistakes in subject-verb agreement:

Two subjects connected by *and* are plural. Two subjects connected by *or* are singular

Jane and Jim are going to the movies.

Jane or Jim is going to the store to get milk.

There is never the subject of a sentence. If a sentence begins with *there*, it is inverted. Match your verb with the subject that follows.

There **are five main categories**.

There **is one way** to get to that conclusion.

2. Make sure your pronouns agree in number and form with the nouns they replace.

    Each child is entitled to **his or her** own book.

    not

    Each child is entitled to **their** own book.

    The pronoun refers to one child, therefore it must be singular. Avoid using *their* as the all-purpose pronoun. It is common in spoken English today, but sloppy and unacceptable when you are writing an academic paper.

3. If you make comparisons, they must be like in form.

   The **standards** of achievement in Japan are greater than **those** in our country.

   not

   The **standards** of achievement in Japan are greater than our country.

4. Make sure any modifying words or phrases are as close to the words or phrase they modify as possible. This will avoid any confusion.

   Heading back to court, John felt the sting of the wind on his neck.

   not

   Heading back to court, the wind stung **John's** neck.

   Who was heading back to court, John or the wind?

ACADEMIC OR FORMAL WRITING

If you are writing a formal research paper, there is a certain tone you are expected to take. There are times when you'll be writing papers in which you want to use a relaxed voice, but, in general, there are a few guidelines you are expected to follow:

1. Don't use the pronoun *you*. *One* is more acceptable for academic writing. It may sound awkward to you at first, but let us warn you that most professors will cringe if you refer to your reader as *you*. For example:

   Acceptable: When one reads the translator's introduction to Kierkegaard's *Fear and Trembling*, one gets important information about Walter Lowrie's sense of the work.

Unacceptable: When you read the translator's introduction to Kierkegaard's *Fear and Trembling,* you get important information about Walter Lowrie's sense of the work.

2. Don't use contractions. In general, contractions are considered less formal.

   Acceptable: He would not, in fact he could not, compromise his integrity in this way.

   Unacceptable: He wouldn't, in fact he couldn't, compromise his integrity in this way.

3. Don't use *I* too frequently. While you may have a few sentences in which you are expressly stating your opinion, you should keep your tone more formal and less personal.

   Acceptable: The research showed that Jones was more competent than was anticipated.

   Unacceptable: I found that Jones was more competent than I had anticipated.

NUMBERS, ABBREVIATIONS, FOREIGN TERMS

For the most part, numbers should be written out up to one hundred. For example:

There were thirty-three women at the party.

The tally was 1,569 for passage.

Spell out any round numbers, such as one thousand, two million, and so forth, as long as they can be expressed in two words. If not, use a combination of numbers and words: 4.5 billion, 65 million. If you have a series of numbers, it is acceptable to use the numbers:

We found 6 bones, 7 fragments, and 12 pieces of glass at the site.

Use numbers to refer to dates, with the exception of decades and centuries:

The conflict was resolved in 1974.

The nineties were a tumultuous time.

The nineteenth century was a period during which many great English novels were written.

In less formal reports, you may refer to a decade or a year this way:

The 1970s marked the end of an era.

He was happy to go to his reunion for the Class of '75. (Use an apostrophe to indicate that part of the date has been omitted.)

For the most part, spell out things in your text that you might commonly abbreviate, unless the term is really quite unwieldy.

Preferred: John was to arrive at two in the afternoon.

Not preferred: John was to arrive at two p.m.

Preferred: Henrietta found her way up to Alaska.

Not preferred: Henrietta found her way up to AK.

but:

Preferred: The USSR was soon dissolved.

Not Preferred: The Union of Soviet Socialist Republics was soon dissolved.

Preferred: It was then that Russell earned his Ph.D.

Not Preferred: It was then that Russell earned his doctorate of philosophy.

Check your dictionary if you are not sure how to abbreviate something properly; if you're still in doubt, write it out the long way. When you are writing your bibliography or citations, it is perfectly acceptable to abbreviate.

If you use any foreign words, they must be reproduced as they appear in their language—that means with accents and such. For example: cliché or raison d'être. In general, you should underline (or italicize) foreign words and phrases, but there are many exceptions to this rule. You don't need to underline quotations, titles that are in quotations (rather than underlined), names and words (such as cliché or raison d'être) that are so commonly used as to be assimilated into our language.

TIP

If the foreign word appears in the dictionary, you don't need to italicize.

Consult an English language dictionary if you are unsure.

RESPECTFUL AND NONSEXIST LANGUAGE

Careful, considerate writers are always aware of topics and terms that have a negative connotation, or that exclude members of your audience. When referring to ethnic groups, we recommend highly that you avoid terms that are anything less than respectful and professional. If your sources are of the highest caliber, you should have no problem letting them guide you as to terminology. If your intentions are to write an educated paper, using any less will compromise your goal.

The issue of nonsexist language is certainly more highly charged. Many of the terms suggested seem overly cumbersome or extreme. However, we have found that it takes only a moderate amount of effort to use terms that are not offensive. Here are some general guidelines for you to follow.

Pronouns

Once upon a time, any time an author substituted a singular pronoun for a noun of indeterminate sex, it was *he*. For example:

> If a doctor is concerned about rising medical
> costs, **he** should consult our firm.

This was especially true whenever traditional "male" occupations were used : doctor, lawyer, judge, executive, and so on. It seemed the only time you'd see *she* used was the reference was to a more traditionally "female" role:

> If a secretary wants to improve **her** skills, **she** should buy this book.

The problem? The author, perhaps without even trying to, has perpetuated inaccurate stereotypes, something we all wish to avoid. There are several solutions to the sticky pronoun dilemma.

1. Especially in academic papers, *he or she* (as long as it is used sparingly) makes an appropriate substitute:

    Acceptable: If an executive inspires his or her people, the company's productivity will be higher.

    However, avoid excessive use:

    Unacceptable: If an executive inspires his or her people, he or she will see his or her company's productivity increase.

2. Use the plural.

    Acceptable: If executives inspire their people, their companies' productivity will increase.

3. Reword the whole sentence.

    Acceptable: If an executive inspires people, the company's productivity will increase.

4. Alternate male and female pronouns as long as it is clear what your references are.

    Acceptable: The most important rule a student needs to consider is clarity. Is his point well made? Does she feel the audience is satisfied?

5. Use the pronoun *one*. While the use of *one* as a pronoun may sound unnatural in real life, it is acceptable for use in an academic paper. As with *he or she*, try not to overuse it—it will overwhelm your sentence.

> **Acceptable:** The most important rule one needs to consider is clarity. Is one's point well made? Does one feel the audience is satisfied?

Man Oh Man!

While the word *man* is used to connote both the male human and humans in general, it is better to avoid the term where possible. Instead of *mankind*, why not use *humanity* or *people*? These words are no more cumbersome that the original and express your idea just as clearly. While we do not advocate the dogmatic slicing of any term that may be even slightly objectionable, we do believe that most terms are easily substituted.

These terms may seem awkward to you at first, but many are becoming part of our everyday language. Do your best to incorporate correct language in your writing. It will go a long way toward making you sound more professional and academic.

Instead of . . .	How about?
Man has evolved through time.	People have evolved through time. Humans have evolved through time.
The best man for the job	The best person for the job
manmade	manufactured or machine-made
the common man	the average person
man-hours	staff-hours
chairman	chair, presiding officer
businessman	executive
mailman	mail carrier
fireman	firefighter
policeman	police officer
congressman	congressional representative

MORE RULES FOR GOOD WRITING

There are many rules for good writing. First of all, there is no easier way to make a bad impression than by using the wrong word in the wrong place. You may notice that we have a very short section on spelling. Most of you are using word-processing programs with spell checkers. What spell checkers don't correct, however, are those circumstances in which you are using the wrong word. Take a look at the following example:

> The reader can notice that the comparisons among the two composers is misleading.

Can you spot the error in that sentence? Actually, there are two errors in that sentence. First of all, the sentence should begin "The reader *may* notice . . ." The word *can* means *is able to* as opposed to *might*. Do you really want to say that your reader is able to notice the comparisons? The second error is that the sentence should read "the comparisons *between* the two composers. . ." The word *among* is used when you refer to groups of three or more. When you are referring to two people, the correct word is *between*.

These types of errors are all too common. They are easy to make if you are not careful when you write, but more importantly, when you proofread. The following is a list of words that are commonly confused and misused. Be sure you know the differences between (or among) them. We give a sentence for each that should clarify the issue for you.

accept/except

I *accept* your challenge.

Everyone was able to go *except* me.

affect/effect

The movie *affected* me greatly.

The *effect* of all that beautiful music was inspiring.

allusion/illusion

The paper was filled with literary *allusions*.

I have no *illusion* that Professor Harper will pass me this term.

alternate/alternative

Marie *alternated* shifts with Paolo; every other week, she took evenings and he took days.

There are only a few *alternatives* to meat that are as high in protein.

ambiguous/ambivalent
Professor Smith warned us to be clear, not *ambiguous*, in the statement of our theses.

I'm still feeling *ambivalent* about whether to write about Monet or Manet.

between/among
Between the two of us, Mary is the stronger.

Among the students in the class, Roger is the smartest.

bring/take
Bring the book to me.

Take the book away.

can/may
I *can* finally swim! Mary taught me.

"*May* I go to the party with you?"

censor/censure
The panel *censored* the movie by removing all objectionable material before it was released.

The student board decided to *censure* the student for cheating on an exam.

common/mutual
We have a *common* purpose. (meaning *shared purpose*)

We have a *mutual* attraction. (meaning a *reciprocal attraction*)

compliment/complement
Dean Smith *complimented* my ability to get to class on time.

Mashed potatoes are the perfect *complement* to roast beef.

continual/continuous
The students formed a *continuous* line that surrounded the building in protest of its demolition.

The program was interrupted every few minutes by a *continual* banging in the pipes.

emigrate/immigrate
People *emigrated* from Ireland to the United States.

They *immigrated* to our country to escape great famine in their own.

eminent/immanent/imminent
The author is the *eminent* source in the field of physics.

The *immanent* faith of St. Theresa of Avila is what makes her so appealing.

The due date for that paper is *imminent*.

farther/further

It is *farther* to drive to Florida than to Maryland.

I hope to *further* my discussion of Kierkegaard in the next paper I write.

fewer/less

We ordered *fewer* sheets of paper from the store this time.

I have *less* work to do.

former/latter

I have two classes on Tuesday: biology and aerobics. The *former* is in the science building, but the *latter* is in the fieldhouse.

fortuitous/fortunate

It was *fortuitous* to find that book on the shelf—it was exactly what I needed.

I was *fortunate* to get into the intro art history class—it's almost always full.

greater/greatest

I hope that this score is *greater* than the last.

I must receive the *greatest* score of the group to maintain my status.

healthy/healthful

I hope to eat a *healthful* diet while away at school.

Marina always works better when she is *healthy*.

implicit/explicit

The tone of his voice made it *implicit* to the class that poor work would not be tolerated.

Professor Jones *explicitly* stated that we were not to write one word over three pages for that assignment.

incredible/incredulous

It was an *incredible* sight: an ape rescuing a small child.

The crowd was *incredulous*: They were sure the ape would harm the child.

infer/imply

Marta *implied* that Gene had gained weight when she asked him if those pants were tight.

Gene *inferred* that Martha was a pretty tactless person.

its/it's

A dog likes to have a place to call *its* own: a pillow, dog bed or corner.

It's important to feed your pet every day.

lie/lay

I need to *lie* down after that crazy day.

I *lay* the book down in the hallway.

libel/slander

Roseanne was foolish not to sue that tabloid for *libel* when they printed that story about her.

The speaker *slandered* several of her colleagues that night when she gave a scathing indictment of the new departmental policy.

most/more

Of the ten books we read for our literature class, I enjoyed *Jane Eyre* the *most*.

Of the two books I read this week, I enjoyed *Jane Eyre more*.

respectfully/respectively

Ginger had been taught to bow *respectfully* when her elders entered the room.

I hope to meet Jim and John, *respectively*, to iron out this problem.

their/they're/there

We want to meet Milo and Otto after class in *their* dorm room.

They're not going to be happy that we are there.

There is a way to find the answer to your problem.

your/you're

This is *your* paper, so write it from *your* perspective.

If *you're* going to write this paper, you should do a good job.

GOOD GRAMMAR—A FINAL WORD

This review was simply to acquaint you with some of the fundamentals of good writing. A few pages of review does not a writer make, however. To become adept at writing, you need to practice, to study writing, and to read. As for the practice part—well, you'll be getting a lot of that as you write papers throughout your academic career. As for reading, we assume you'll be doing a good deal of that as well. And as far as studying goes, there are certain books we recommend, if you feel the inclination to go further.

The Elements of Style   Strunk and White

This little book has graced the shelves of college students for generations. We stress the word little, because what is so wonderful about it is its brevity. The important points of style are presented clearly and eloquently.

Writing Smart   Marcia Lerner

A entertaining and interesting guide to writing, whether fiction or lab reports. Learning how to write well doesn't have to be boring.

A Dictionary of Modern English Usage, Second Edition H.W. Fowler

This guide goes through all the nuts and bolts and nuances of language. A third edition has recently been released to mixed reviews. While it has been completely updated, if you're a stickler for grammar, the second edition is considered a classic.

SPELLING AND PUNCTUATION

LEARNING HOW TO SPELL CORRECTLY

Since most of you are working on a word processor, it seems silly to spend too much time on spelling. Your word-processing program will spell check items for you. However, spelling is not a completely lost art. There *are* words that are not in the spell checker's dictionary. You may be using alternate spellings of words. The following brief section is to remind you about some basics of spelling correctly.

Good spelling doesn't mean knowing how to spell everything. It means recognizing misspelled words. How do you do that? There are two steps:

1. **Read.** The more you read, the better your spelling will become. This is especially true as you use more and more difficult words in your writing. Good spelling, as we pointed out, means recognizing bad spelling. The more you read certain words, the more you will recognize when they look wrong. It's like learning to listen to music—you can train your ear to discern the good from the bad.

2. **Edit.** Get in the habit of rereading your work and looking up words that the spell checker doesn't pick up. Remember, your spell checker will not help you if you misspell a word and inadvertently turn it into another word. You need to develop the skill of knowing when words look wrong. Never hand something in until you have checked it. The more you edit, the better your paper will be.

DON'T DON'T DON'T MISSPELL ON PURPOSE!

Please remember that you are writing a paper—not a note to your friend. Don't use silly spellings like *nite* instead of *night* or abbreviations that are not commonly used. These kind of silly spellings only compromise the seriousness of your work. Also, keep in mind that misspelled words may cost you credit on a paper.

Punctuation

Correct punctuation, like correct grammar, makes your paper easy to read and seamless. Incorrect punctuation will confuse your reader and look sloppy. You want a reader to understand your words, not obsess about your commas—especially when the reader is a professor who is grading you. Use this quick guide to punctuation as a reference if you're not sure when to use a colon and when to use a semicolon. We will give more detailed instruction on punctuation within citations in the next chapter.

If you are writing fiction, you have a lot more latitude to be creative in your use of language and punctuation. In an academic paper, however, you should attempt to adhere to the rules as much as you can.

Have we still not convinced you? Take a look at these two sentences:

> Frida Kahlo, the painter, lived with Diego Rivera.

> Frida Kahlo, the painter lived with Diego Rivera.

In the first sentence, we are telling the reader a fact about Frida Kahlo. In the second, you might think that we are telling Frida Kahlo about a painter who's living with Diego Rivera. The words in each sentence are exactly the same. Incorrect punctuation makes the second sentence needlessly ambiguous.

Periods

1. Use a period when you are coming to a complete stop after a statement or a command.

   Monet was a famous Impressionist painter.

   Descartes was known as a mathematician and philosopher.

2. Use a period after most abbreviations. Monograms, government organizations, television or radio networks, and post

office state abbreviations don't need periods. You don't need to add a second period if the abbreviation comes at the end of the sentence; one will do double duty.

Prof. Smolenski
Mme. Francez
Oct. 16
3 a.m.
CBS, WBCI, KZOO, CIA, JFK
We will meet the committee at 4 p.m.

3. If the words inside of the parentheses are not a full sentence, put the period at the end of the sentence (like this). If, however, the words in the parentheses are a full sentence, put the period inside the parentheses. (For example, a sentence like this has a period inside the parenthesis.)

4. Put a period inside quotation marks.

In his famous speech, Martin Luther King, Jr. told his listeners, "I have a dream."

The note on the dean's door said "Don't knock unless you have important business."

5. Use periods after all the letters and numbers for an outline, unless they are in parentheses:

I.
   A.
   B.
II.
   A.
   B.
      1.
      2.
         a.
         b.
            (1)
            (2)

Commas

Commas are used to put a pause in the reader's mind. If, while speaking, you would pause at a certain point in a sentence, put a comma there. When in doubt, read your sentences out loud. Too many or too few commas can muddle your meaning.

1. Use a comma to separate two independent clauses connected by *and, but, or, nor, for*.

   The beginning of the situation called for tact, but we soon found that a bold approach was better.

   The Galapagos Islands are a haven for many species, and they are a tourist attraction for the adventurous naturalist.

   If the clauses are short enough, you may leave out the comma.

   Lincoln was elected and he was successful.

   Mozart was unhappy but he was working.

2. Use commas to separate items in a list. You should put a comma before the last *and*.

   Among the many hats worn by Benjamin Franklin were inventor, writer, and politician.

3. Use a comma to set off an introductory phrase from a sentence.

   Trying too hard to detach from nature, modern people sit in glass towers of sorts.

   More astonishing owing to its uniformity than diversity, planet Earth is a marvel to study.

4. Use commas to separate a list of adjectives if you could use *and* between them.

The form of the Japanese haiku is a short, structured, beautiful one.

(You would say ". . is a short *and* structured *and* beautiful one.")

Don't use a comma if you wouldn't use the word *and*.

Wedgewood's trademark was a light-blue pottery.

(You wouldn't say ". . . was a light and blue pottery.")

5. Use a comma to separate out the name of a person you are addressing, or a person's title.

The split occurred when the ambassador's secretary, Jones, informed him of the turmoil.

Alexander Solzhenitsyn, Nobel–prizewinning Russian novelist, was exiled for his critical study of the Soviet penal system.

6. Use a comma to set off a group of words that contrast your main point.

Louis XIV was flawed, not perfect, in his vision of the monarchy.

I intend to prove that, far from difficult, classical music is quite simple to understand.

7. Use a comma to set apart the figures in a date, and the parts of an address (not between the state and the zip code, however.)

December 6, 1945

Anywhere, Ohio 44445

8. Use a comma to separate hundreds, thousands, millions, and each three digits after.

9,876,543,210

9. And, last but not least, use a comma if you need to pause or to set aside a group of words to make your meaning clear. This is the discretionary use of a comma; don't overdo it.

Maud died in Normandy, after an illustrious life.

rather than

Maud died in Normandy after an illustrious life.

The Question Mark

1. Use a question mark to show that a direct question is being asked.

Did Montaigne recognize his own greatness?

You don't need a question mark for an indirect question.

Washington wondered if he would ever find a solution.

2. Put the question mark inside quotation marks if the quotation is a question. Put the question mark outside the quotes if the quote itself is not a question.

"Are you—Nobody—too?" asked Emily Dickinson. (The quote is a question.)

Do you know who said "Neither a borrower nor a lender be." ? (The quote is not a question.)

The Exclamation Point

While it may be fun to use exclamation points, they almost never have a place in an academic paper. Compare:

> Kant was a genius!

> to

> Kant was a genius.

As you can see, the exclamation point usually makes a serious statement sound like a high school cheer. If you feel you must use an exclamation point, please, only one; never, ever use more than one exclamation point at the end of a sentence. (None of this, please!!!)

1. Use an exclamation point if you are expressing a strong statement or sentiment.

   Jones wanted to go more than anything!

2. Use an exclamation after an interjection.

   Wow! The results were impressive.

The Semicolon

Semicolons are tricky. Most people don't use them correctly. But, the correct use of a semicolon can be very impressive. Once you know the rules, you'll be using them all the time with confidence. They are a nice middleground between the full stop of a period and the pause of a comma.

1. Use a semicolon when you have two independent clauses that are not joined by a conjunction. Think of it this way: If you can separate the parts into two full sentences, a semicolon can be used.

   Ownership of land is associated with the female Hopi; the rights to own are passed through the mother in the family.

   His work was vindicated; his reputation was intact.

   I came; I saw; I conquered.

2. Use a semicolon if you have a long list of names with commas in them and therefore a comma would not be clear enough to separate them.

   The committee was made up of the Prof. Jane Velasquez, head of the English department; Dean Peter Jones, dean of students; Dr. Mary Martina, professor emeritus; and a student representative from each class.

The Colon

1. Use a colon to introduce a list.

   There are several ways to reach that stage: practice, take lessons, work with others.

2. Use a colon to introduce a quote.

   William Shakespeare said: "And my kingdom for a little grave, A little little grave, an obscure grave."

3. Use a colon to introduce an explanation.

   The scientists had a good reason for wanting the additional funding: they were on the brink of discovery.

Quotation Marks

Quotations are typically used extensively in research papers. We will go into the rules of how to incorporate them and cite them in your paper in the section about quotations. Here, we simply go through the rules for the use of quotation marks when writing.

1. Use quotation marks for a direct quote. Put any commas or periods inside the quotation marks. Put question marks and exclamation marks inside the quotation marks if they are part of the quote; put them outside if they are not.

"Remember the Alamo!"

"Don't forget to call," said Alexander Graham Bell's mother.

Can you imagine what drove Abraham Lincoln to state: "A house divided will not stand." ?

2. Quotation marks may be used to show irony. However, like exclamation points, this type of writing rarely is legitimate in an academic venue. Use it sparingly, if at all, and only in less formal writing.

   Michelle "borrowed" my homework so that she could copy it.

3. Quotations may go on for more than one paragraph. If that is the case, you should put a new set of marks at the beginning of the new paragraph, but *not* at the end of the old paragraph. For example:

   John told his story: "We were going to prove the theory that when a stream could no longer widen a channel, it would deepen it. We gathered together a class and went to the Downy River.

   "It was a beautiful day, but we were not to have success. First, we had a flat tire, then we got lost. By the time we got to the stream it was almost dark. Perhaps next time."

4. You don't need quotation marks for an indirect quote.

   It was Einstein who said that imagination is more important than genius.

   At the end of her acceptance speech, Sally remembered to say thank you to her parents.

Parentheses

1. Use parentheses to set off anything extra that would otherwise interrupt your sentence.

   John Maynard Keynes (an economist) was the founder of Keynesian theory.

2. As we mentioned before, put a period inside the parentheses if you have a complete sentence. Otherwise, put the period outside the parentheses. Don't put a comma after the parentheses unless you would use one anyway.

Dashes

1. Dashes are optional. Some people love to use dashes—others don't. Dashes are used to set off a phrase, similarly to commas or parentheses.

   You may want to read about the Brontes—a group of highly talented sisters—or you may choose to read their novels.

   instead of

   You may want to read about the Brontes, a group of highly talented sisters, or you may choose to read their novels.

   When Marty entered the room—with a little trepidation—he found that it was in perfect order.

   instead of

   When Marty entered the room (with a little trepidation) he found that it was in perfect order.

CAPITALIZATION AND PUNCTUATION OF TITLES

When writing a title in your list of cited works, or anywhere in the body of the paper, you must adhere to certain rules. The first question is: Exactly what is the title? This may seem silly, but it is not uncommon for the title of a work to vary from the cover to the title page. If there is any discrepancy, use the title as it appears on the title page of the document.

When you are writing the citation, there are rules for how the title is to be capitalized. Do *not* pay attention to the way the title is capitalized in the card catalog or online catalog. The rules for capitalization are different for classification purposes. Here are the rules you need to know:

1. Capitalize the first word, and all the principal words in the title and in the subtitle of the document.

2. Do not capitalize any article (*a, an, the*) unless it is the first word in the title.

3. Do not capitalize any preposition (*in, around, between, before*) unless it is the first word in the title.

4. Do not capitalize a conjunction (*and, or, nor, but*) unless it is the first word in the title.

5. Do not capitalize the *to*, if it is part of an infinitive (*to* play, *to* go, *to* see), unless it is the first word in the title.

Samples

Eclipse of God

Reason in History

The Sickness unto Death

Romeo and Juliet

Who Said That?

A Theory of Justice

"I Hear America Sing"

If there is a subtitle, use a colon and a space between the main title and the subtitle. For example:

> Crisis in the Classroom: The Remaking of American Education

> America's Asia: Dissenting Essays in Asian Studies

If the work is an untitled poem, you may use the first line of the poem as the title. Reproduce it as it is written—do not capitalize words unless they are capitalized in the line of the poem.

TITLES: UNDERLINE, ITALICS, OR QUOTATION MARKS?

Titles are underlined whenever the work they represent is or would be published as a separate entity. In other words, if the thing is a whole, not a part, then you would underline the title. This would include a book, a play, a long poem, a pamphlet, a magazine title or a recording or musical composition, for example. You may very well see the titles of these types of publications set in *italics*. Because italics may not print clearly, most professors prefer underlining, which cannot be misinterpreted. However, underlining and italicizing are usually interchangeable.

Examples:

Books:

> *Crime and Punishment*
>
> *The Moor's Last Sigh*
>
> *The Rise of the Meritocracy*

Plays:

> *A Funny Thing Happened on the Way to the Forum*
>
> *A Midsummer Night's Dream*

Long Poems:

> *The Inferno*
>
> *Beowulf*

Pamphlets:

> *The Consumer's Guide to Auto Buying*
>
> *Common Sense*

Newspapers, Magazines, and Journals:

> *The London Times*
>
> *BusinessWeek*
>
> *Race and Reason*

Artwork:

> Michelangelo's *David*
>
> *Guernica* by Pablo Picasso

Movies:

> *Citizen Kane*
>
> *Star Wars*

Use quotation marks for titles whenever what they represent is a part of something else. This would include short stories, short poems, articles, chapters from books, episodes from television shows, a song or part of a recording.

Short Stories and Essays:

> "The Frontiers of Criticism"
>
> "The Lottery"

Articles:

> "Marriage Rites in Ancient Persia"
>
> " 'I Don't Want Her in My Home': Bias against African-American Domestic Servants, 1910–1980"

Episode from a television show:

> "The Trouble with Tribbles"

Chapters from books:

"Say You Want a Revolution"

"The Professional Debate"

Songs:

"Blue Skies"

"Summertime"

CHAPTER 4

Style Guide, Part II

Citations

Throughout your paper, you will be citing the different works you have used in your research. As we've stated before, careful citation is the key to avoiding plagiarism. Your note cards will help you to avoid using information without giving credit. There are three ways for you to use information that you've researched:

1. Direct quotation. In this form, you are taking any piece of writing and putting it word for word in the body of your paper.

    Martin Buber believed that "The relationship between religion and reality prevailing in a given epoch is the most accurate index of its true character."

2. Paraphrasing. When you are paraphrasing, you are taking the direct quotation and putting it in your own words.

   Martin Buber believed that we could judge any era's character by the way it related religion and reality.

3. Summary. When you summarize, you take a whole section of material and give a short synopsis of it.

   The central thesis of Buber's first lecture was the relationship between religion and reality.

In each of these three cases, you must be sure to let your reader know from which book and from where in the book your information came.

Quotations

At some point during your work, you will almost certainly want to use a quote. And well you should—quotes are wonderful ways to punch up a paper. Many beginning writers, however, fall into the trap of overusing quotations. Be careful: Too many quotes will make your paper look unoriginal, or like you are simply trying to fill space. Effective quotation, like anything, depends on judicious use.

First, let's run through the rules of how to use a quotation in the body of your paper.

Rule #1

You must quote *exactly*. After all, this is a quotation, not a paraphrase. If you must leave out a few words from the middle of your quote, use the ellipsis (three dots with a space before and after each . . .) to indicate that words have been removed. Sometimes you must change a word or two to clarify a quote pulled out of context or to make it blend more smoothly into the body of the paper. Any word that has been changed from the original or added for clarity must be bracketed: [ ].

You have an obligation, however, to retain the integrity of the original document. This isn't a movie poster: Pulling the word *tremendous* out of a quote that reads "this movie was a tremendous failure" isn't ethical in the academic world. Use the ellipses and brackets carefully and with respect.

Exact quote:

> "If there is one word on which we can fix, which will suggest the maximum of what I mean by the term 'a classic', it is the word *maturity*." (T.S. Eliot, "What is a Classic," *On Poetry and Poets.* [1948; New York: Farrar, Straus & Giroux] 54)

Incorporating a phrase from the quote into your text:

> T.S. Eliot writes about the term "classic," with the suggestion that the reader focus on one word, "the word *maturity*."

Words omitted with writer's additions:

> When Eliot defines the word "classic," he offers the following caution: "If there is only one word on which we can fix . . . it is the word *maturity*."

Words changed:

> "If there is one word on which we can fix, which will suggest the maximum of what [Eliot means] by the term 'a classic,' it is the word *maturity*."

If the omitted words come at the end of the sentence, you have to incorporate a period into the ellipsis. Use four dots, with no space before the first or after the last. We will use the following quote:

> "Those who arrived from West Indian nations were usually legal, but the quotas for other Western Hemisphere countries were too low to handle the increasing numbers of émigrés." (Alana J. Erickson, " 'I Don't Want Her in My Home': Bias against African-American Domestic Servants, 1910–1980," *Race and Reason* 1996–7)

> Erickson writes that "Those who arrived from
> West Indian nations were usually legal. . . ."

If you have a citation in parentheses after the ellipsis at the end of the quote, put the period after the citation:

> Erickson writes that "Those who arrived from
> West Indian nations were usually legal . . ." (31).

You do not need the ellipses if you are just taking a phrase from the quote:

> Erickson notes that this particular group was
> "usually legal."

Rule #2

If you have four lines or fewer of quotation, just incorporate them into the body of your paper. If, however, the quote runs to more than four lines, you should indent the quote, ten spaces (one inch) in from the left margin. When you indent in this way, do not use quotation marks. If you are quoting a single paragraph, no further indentation is needed. If you are using more than one paragraph, use a three-space indentation for each paragraph on top of the ten-space indentation.

Rule #3

If you are quoting poetry that is four lines or less, separate the lines with slashes:

> Robert Frost laid claim to that feeling when
> he wrote, "But I have promises to keep,/And
> miles to go before I sleep,/And miles to go
> before I sleep."

If the quote runs longer than four lines, indent as you did for a prose quote:

> Samuel Coleridge's poem "Kubla Khan" was
> written after a dream induced by an opiate
> he had taken:

In Xanadu did Kubla Khan

A stately pleasure-dome
decree:

Where Alph, the sacred
river, ran

Through caverns measure-
less to man

Down to a sunless sea.

BIBLIOGRAPHIES

There are many different ways to reference your citations. Most academic institutions require or accept MLA (Modern Language Association) style documentation. While the traditional style (sometimes called "Chicago Style") uses footnotes to cite specific texts, MLA style cites a text in parentheses right in the body of your paper. This eliminates the need for footnotes. The reader can then refer to the Works Cited list at the end of your paper to get the full citation (author, title, etc.) You will find, in general, that most professors are simply looking to see that you have used an accepted method for citing documents, and that you are consistent in that method.

There are several ways you may title the section of your report in which you document the literature you've used. Depending on which style of documentation you use, you may call it a *Bibliography, List of Works Cited, Literature Cited,* or simply *Works Cited.* Some professors may ask you to compile an annotated bibliography. This is just what it sounds like: A bibliography with a short abstract about the work you've used for research. The annotation is typically about two to five sentences.

You may also have to compile a *List of Works Consulted* that would include sources that you read for your research but did not ever specifically cite in your report. We will give examples of all the different types of bibliographic information you may have to compile at the end of this section. First, let's go through the mechanics of how each entry is written.

No matter what type of documentation you provide, there are a few general guidelines you need to follow. First of all, bibliographies are always arranged alphabetically by author. If there is no author credited, use the title of the work, alphabetizing by the first main word (excluding the articles *a, an* or *the*).

If your research is vast, your professor may ask you to divide the works-cited list by chronology or subject matter. You will certainly be told if you are expected to arrange your bibliography in other than a standard way.

The list should always be at the end of your paper. Always begin on a new page—don't start it on the last page of your writing. If you have any notes or table, the bibliography will follow those. The page numbers should follow the page numbers of your document. Don't start new page numbers for the bibliography, or leave out page numbers.

The title *List of Works Cited* or *Bibliography* should be centered at the top of the list, one inch from the top of the page. Each entry should begin at your right margin; indent five spaces if the entry is longer than one line. The list should be double-spaced throughout. Here are some examples of how to write bibliographic entries for a variety of sources. You will note that we italicize titles in the entries that follow. Just to reiterate: italicizing and underlining titles of various works are usually interchangeable; check to see whether your professor has a preference.

One Author Book

This is the simplest and most straightforward type of bibliographic entry. The same form should be used for a pamphlet. It follows the form:

> Author's last name, first name. *Title.* City
> of publication: Publisher, date of publi-
> cation.

For example:

> Davis, Kenneth C. *Don't Know Much about*
> *History.* New York: Avon Books, 1990.

Always use the author's name as it appears on the title page. If the author uses initials, use initials. If the name is given in full, write it out. If you feel it is necessary to add to the author's name as it appears, you must bracket the information you've added. Perhaps, for example, you have referred to T.S. Eliot as Thomas throughout your work.

Eliot, T.S.

Eliot, T[homas] S[tearns]

Use the subtitle if it appears on the title page:

Jahoda, Gloria. *The Trail of Tears: The Story of the American Indian Removal 1813–1855.* New York: Holt, Rinehardt and Winston, 1975.

You may exclude any degrees or affiliations that an author has. If his name is followed by Ph.D., Sir, Lord, President, or Saint, there is no need to include this in the entry. If, however the author is a Jr., Sr., or IV, you should add this determinant in the name of clarity: You need to distinguish a Sr., from a Jr. Put a comma after the author's first name and add the abbreviated suffix, followed by a period:

Kennedy, John F., Jr.

Get the publication information from the title page of the book. If there is more than one city listed, use only the first. You don't need to write the country or state, unless the city might be unknown to your reader. If you are supplying information not found in the book (the city of publication, for example), bracket it. This will show your reader that it is extra information you are providing. If you cannot, after a valiant search, find a piece of information (the date of publication, for example), just note it with one of the following abbreviations:

- n.d for no date,

- n.p. for no place of publication, or

- n.p. for no publisher

Second Entry By The Same Author

If you use two or more works by the same author, you don't need to write the author's name each successive time. Just use three dashes in a row in place of the author's name.

For example:

> Howard, Philip. *New Words for Old*. London:
> Hamish Hamilton, 1977.

> ———. *The State of the Language*. London:
> Penguin Books, 1986.

This means that the second book, *The State of the Language*, was authored by Philip Howard as well.

Author as Editor

If the work is a compilation or anthology, the "author" is considered to be whoever edited or compiled the work. Check out the name on the title page. That's the name you should use as the author of the work. You need to indicate what the author was responsible for (editing, translating, etc.). Follow the author name by a comma and the job description as indicated on the title page. Use the abbreviation *ed.* for editor and *comp.* for compiler. If the author both edited and translated, for example, list both functions—ed. and trans. See the next section for dealing with more than one editor, compiler, and/or translator. If the author is the same as the previous entry, use the dashes as mentioned in the last section, follow with a comma and description.

> Thoms, W.J., ed. *A Collection of Early English
> Prose Romances*. London: Pickering, 1858.

> Rossiter, Clinton, ed. *The Federalist Papers:
> Hamilton, Madison and Jay*. New York:
> Mentor, 1961.

> Stampp, Kenneth M. *The Peculiar Institution:
> Slavery in the Ante-Bellum South*. New
> York: Knopf, 1956.

> ———, ed. *The Causes of the Civil War*. New
> York: Spectrum Books / Prentice-Hall,
> 1974.

More Than One Author

Here, you don't need to alphabetize the authors if there is more than one. Use the order as given on the title page. The first name will appear last name first, first name last, but subsequent names go in regular order. Place a comma after each author name, before the *and*. If the authors have some other function—editors or compilers, follow the names with a comma and the appropriate abbreviation.

> X, Malcolm, with Alex Haley. *The Autobiography of Malcolm X*. New York: Grove, 1964.

> Hackworth, David H., and Julie Sherman. *About Face: The Odyssey of an American Warrior*. New York: Simon and Schuster, 1989.

> Rousseau, G.S., and Roy Porter, eds. *Exoticism in the Enlightenment*. Manchester: Manchester University Press, 1990.

If you have more than one author and the first one listed is already in your bibliography, do *not* replace her name with three dashes, as before. Write out the name in full the next time if it is part of a group:

> Fowler, H.W. *A Dictionary of Modern English Usage*, 2nd ed., revised by Sir Ernest Gowers. Oxford: Clarendon Press, 1965.

> Fowler, H.W., and F.G. Fowler. *The King's English*. Oxford: Oxford University Press, 1931.

You have the option of only using the first author's name followed by a comma and the Latin term *et al* (meaning "and others") if there are more than three authors. Even though it may be cumbersome, you still may choose to write out the names of all the authors. This may be important if you want your reader to note the third or fourth author listed.

Deere, Carmen, et al. *In the Shadows of the Sun: Caribbean Development Alternatives and U.S. Policy.* Boulder: Westview Press, 1990.

Corporate Authors

You may not see a specific author listed on the title page of the work you are using. Often, large companies or associations will publish works under their own name. Use the name of the association, group, or committee as it is listed on the cover page. Specific rules for government publications follow.

American Bar Association. *A Portable Guide to Federal Conspiracy Law: Developing Strategies for Criminal and Civil Cases.* Chicago: PPM of the American Bar Association, 1997.

If the work is a government publication, the rules become more complicated. As above, the agency that sponsored the work is considered the author in the absence of an author credit. First, however, you must identify the country or state of the government. You may abbreviate the name of the organization if it would be clear to the reader.

United States. U.S. Government Services Administration. *How to Buy Surplus Personal Property from the Department of Defense.* Pueblo: GSA, 1992. United States.

Centers for Disease Control and Prevention. *Emerging Infectious Diseases.* Atlanta: National Center for Infectious Disease, 1997.

Parts of a Whole

If the work you are citing is a part of some larger work—a short story or essay from a collection, a poem, or a selection from a book that is written by a different author, you should follow the format:

> Author's last name, first name. "Title of Short
> Piece." Trans. or ed. if applicable. *Title
> of the Book from Which the Piece Comes.*
> Ed. or Comp. of the Book. Place of
> Publication: Publisher, date of publica-
> tion. Pages of the piece cited.

> Camus, Albert. "The Myth of Sisyphus." *The
> Myth of Sisyphus and Other Essays.* Trans.
> Justin O'Brien. New York: Knopf, 1955.
> 54–55.

> Parfit, Derek. "Personal Identity." *Philosophy
> as It Is.* Ed. Ted Honderich and Myles
> Burnyeat. New York: Penguin, 1979. 183–
> 211.

The same basic rules apply if your reference is an encyclopedia
or dictionary. But there are a few differences. You don't need to
name the editor of the work, unless it is a lesser-known reference
work. Some entries are signed; if so, use that as the author name.
If the entry is unsigned, use the title of the entry first. If the work
is arranged alphabetically, page and volume numbers are unnecessary.

> Bradley, James. "Bowery Savings Bank." *The
> Encyclopedia of New York City.* Ed. Kenneth
> T. Jackson. New Haven: Yale University
> Press: New York: The New York Histori-
> cal Society, 1995.

If you are using a familiar ready reference source, such as
Webster's Dictionary, or the *Encyclopedia Britannica*, you do not
need to put in all the publication information, just the edition
and year of publication.

> "Revolutionary War in America." *World Book
> Encyclopedia.* 1995 ed.

Introductions, Prefaces, etc.

If the cited reference is the foreword or afterword to a book,
treat it as a part of the whole. The difference here is that you

need only identify the part as introduction or foreword, etc. Do not use quotation marks or underlining. If the pages are Roman numerals instead of numbers, write the page numbers as they appear.

> Matthews, John. Foreword. *The Encyclopedia of Arthurian Legends*. By Ronan Coghlan. Shaftesbury, Dorset: Element, 1991. iii–iv.

If the author of the foreword or afterword is the same as the author of the book, you only need to use the last name when noting the primary author.

> Perelman, Ch[aim]. Introduction. *The New Rhetoric: A Treatise on Argumentation*. By Perelman and L. Olbrechts-Tyteca. Trans. John Wilkinson and Purcell Weaver. Notre Dame: University of Notre Dame Press, 1969. v–vi.

Cross-Referencing

You don't need to repeat the full name of the work if you have more than one selection from it. A cross-reference uses the names of the main authors, editors or compilers of the book. For example:

> Brouwer, Norman, J. "South Street Seaport." Jackson 1099.

> Jackson, Kenneth T. Preface. Jackson xi-xiv.

> Tobias, Marilyn. "Sullivan and Cromwell." Jackson 11-41.

If there is any specific information about the piece you are citing—if it was translated, for example—write it in after the title of the piece.

Who Wrote It?

If the author is anonymous, just use the title as the entry. Alphabetize by the first important word in the title. If the author's name or the date of publication is not given in the work you are citing, but you are supplying it, put this information in brackets.

> "Confessions of an Erstwhile Child." *The New Republic.* 15 June 1974: 11-13.

Different Editions

Many books are published in different editions. Sometimes there is a paperback edition as well as a hardcover edition. Some famous works are published over and over again. Think of how many editions of the Bible there are. There may be different translations, new printings that are illustrated, and so forth. Clearly, it is important to let the reader know which edition of the work you are referring to.

Frequently, the name of the translator or editor will be enough to identify the edition you are using. Put the author's name first, then title, then after the period write *Ed.* (for *edited by*) or *Trans.* (for *translated by*) with the editor or translator's name. You have the option of putting the original year of publication right after the title. Use this form, omitting the information you do not have:

> Original Author's Last Name, First Name. *Title of Work.* Original Date of Publication (optional). Ed. Editor's Name. Edition (if available). Place of Publication: Publisher, date of publication (for this edition).

> Yeats, W.B. *A Vision and Related Writings.* 1937. Sel. and ed. by A. Norman Jeffares. London: Arena, 1990.

Use the abbreviations *ed.* for edition, *rev. ed.* for revised edition, *enl. ed.* for enlarged edition, and *abr. ed.* for abridged edition.

> Larkin, Oliver W. *Art and Life in America.* Rev. and enl. ed. New York: Holt, 1960

If the book is a paperback or republished version, put the date of the original publication following the title, before the new publication information. Any other information is optional. You may, for example, add the original publishing information (city of publication and publisher). You should also add any new information; for example, if the book has been supplemented in any way.

> Nash, Gary. *Red, White and Black: The Peopling of Early America.* 1974. New York: Prentice-Hall, 1982.

Publishers' Imprints and More Than One Publisher

Some publishers have special divisions, known as imprints. For example, Vintage is an imprint of Random House. Use the information as it appears on the title page. Hyphenate the imprint name with the main publishing house (Vintage-Random House, for example) *if* both are on the main page. If there is more than one publishing house on the title page, list them all, separated by colons.

More Than One Volume

If you are using more than one volume of a multivolume work, indicate the total number of volumes after the title (and any editor or edition information) and before the publication information. Sometimes the work is published over a period of years—indicate the full range in the publication date.

> *Encyclopedia of World Art.* 15 vols. New York: McGraw-Hill, 1959–68.

If, however, you are only using one volume, just give the specific volume number. You may add the complete number of volumes at the end of the entry if you wish. That information is optional. If you choose to include the complete number of volumes, put it after the date of publication.

> Bryan, William Jennings, ed. *The World's Famous Orations.* Vol. VIII. New York: Funk and Wagnalls Co., 1906.

or

> Bryan, William Jennings, ed. *The World's Famous Orations.* Vol. VIII. New York: Funk and Wagnalls Co., 1906. 10 vols.

If the work is part of a series, indicate the series name before the publication information, neither underlined nor in quotations.

> Farwell, Paul. *Fundamentals of Zen Buddhism.* Religion in Daily Life 4. Chicago: Zen Press, 1995.

Unpublished Material

If the proceedings of a conference or a report are published, treat the source just as you would a book. You may add information after the title, neither underlined nor in quotations, about the nature of the material. If, however, the material is unpublished, be sure to state what it is and where it came from in lieu of publishing data.

> Churchwell, Charles D. "Education for Librarianship in the United States: Some Factors Which Influenced Its Development Between 1919 and 1939." Diss., University of Illinois, Urbana, 1966.

> Columbia University in the City of New York. "Minutes of the Board of Trustees." New York: Columbia University, 1881–1943.

> Municipal Reference Library of the City of New York. "Annual Statistics." New York: Municipal Reference Library of the City of New York, 1914–1918.

> Brooks, Jean, and Betty Maynard. "Final Report to the National Interest Council." Independent Study Project. Dallas: Dallas Public Library, 13 Sept. 1973.

Foreign Titles

There is no difference between citing a foreign book and an English language book, except that you have to figure out what all those words mean. Use the title, place of publication, publisher and author name all as written on the title page. If you feel it is necessary for clarification, put the English translation in brackets.

> Vermes, Genvieve et Josiane Boutet, eds. *France, Pays Multilingue* [France, Multilingual Country]. Vols. I and II. Paris: L'Harmattan, 1987.

Books Published before 1900

You may omit the name of the publisher and include only the place of publication, followed by a comma.

> Dunlop, J.C. *The History of Prose Fiction.* London, 1888.

Periodical Articles

There are a variety of rules for citing articles found in periodicals. The most common type of periodical student use is the academic journal. Here is the basic format:

> Author's Last name, First name. "Title of the Article." *Journal Title* volume number (year of publication): inclusive page numbers.

> Bryden, M.P. "Attentional Strategies and Short-Term Memory in Dichotic Listening." *Cognitive Psychology* 2 (1971): 99–116.

> Corning, W.C. and E. R. John. "Effect of Ribonuclease on Retention of Response in Regenerated Planarians." *Science* 134 (1961): 1363–1365.

You will notice that we haven't included issue numbers, months or seasonal reference (Spring, 1994 for example). That is because in most academic journals pages are numbered consecutively in the volume, which typically coincides with the year. As long as this is the case, issue numbers or months are superfluous. Always check the journal to see how it is numbered, and how the pages are numbered. If an article's pages do not run consecutively, the just write the beginning page number followed by a plus sign (75+).

If the pages within a volume are not numbered consecutively, include the issue number so that your reference can be identified. Just use the format vol:issue. For example, if your reference came from volume 5, issue 3, just write 5:3. If the issues are combined write 5:2–3 (volume 5, issues 2 and 3 combined.) The rest of the citation remains the same.

> Selfridge, O. and U. Neisser. "Pattern Recognition by Machine." *Scientific American* 203:2 (1960): 60–68.

> Cobb, Charles E. "Storm Watch over the Kurils." *National Geographic* 190:4 (1996): 48–67.

If there is no volume number, only issue numbers, use the issue number in place of the volume number, with the same format.

Newspaper Articles

Newspaper article citations are similar to journal citations.

> Author's Last Name, First Name. "Title of the Article." *Name of the Newspaper* [city of publication if it is not in the title] date of publication, edition if applicable: section : page numbers.

TIP

Write the date this way: day month year. Abbreviate any month that is more than four letters long. If your article is continued on another page, you need only write the section and page number of the page it begins on and simply follow it with a + sign.

Eichenwald, Kurt. "U.S. Expands Search of Columbia/HCA in Texas." *New York Times* 21 Mar. 1997: D1+.

Marquand, Robert. "Is Assault by State Official a Civil Rights Violation?" *Christian Science Monitor.* 8 Jan 1997: United States 3+.

If no author is listed, use the title of the article. Omit any article (*a, an* or *the*) from the start of the paper's name. If the piece is an editorial, commentary, or letter, this should be noted after the author's name. You should also note if the letter was a response to a previous letter.

"Charles C. Williamson, 87, Dies: Directed Libraries at Columbia." *New York Times* 13 Jan. 1965. p. 25.

Georgiou, Theodoros. Letter. *Christian Science Monitor* 30 Jan. 1997, opinion/essays: 20.

Reviews

For a review of a work, use this format:

Author's Last Name, First Name. "Title of the Review." Rev. of *Title of the Book Being Reviewed*, by Author of the book being reviewed. *Journal or Newspaper where Review is Found* Date: page numbers.

Blumenthal, Sidney. "The Cold War and the Closet." Rev. of *Whittaker Chambers* by Sam Tanenhaus. *The New Yorker* 17 Mar. 1997: 112–117.

Staples, Brent. "The Master of Monticello." Rev. of *American Sphinx: The Character of Thomas Jefferson*, by Joseph J. Ellis. *New York Times Book Review* 23 Mar. 1997:7.

Magazine Articles

For a magazine article, use the same format as the newspaper article. Use the date on the cover of the issue as the date in your citation. If no author is credited, use the title to alphabetize, using the first primary word.

> Shapiro, Bill. "Can You Improve Your Luck?"
> *Health* Jan./Feb. 1997: 55+

> Carroll, James. "The Silence." *The New Yorker*
> 7 April 1997: 52–69.

Abstract

Since an abstract journal gives a synopsis of information from an article, dissertation or other source, you may wish to cite from it. Simply give all the information for the work cited, just as if you were only citing that, then give the information from the abstract journal. One of the most commonly used abstracts, *Dissertation Abstracts International*, may be abbreviated *DAI*.

> McKee, Nancy Carol. "The Depiction of the Physically Disabled in Preadolescent Contemporary Realistic Fiction Content Analysis." Diss. The Florida State U., 1987. DAI 48 (1987): 240B.

OTHER MEDIA

Television and Radio

Probably the primary difference between referencing a television, radio or film as opposed to a written work is that the title will always come first. Even if you have the name of the writer, it is usually not the primary entry. If the program is an interview, write the name of the interviewee first (last name first, first name last) and the word Interview, neither underlined nor in quotation marks.

"Title of Episode (if applicable)." *Title of Program*. *Title of Series* (if applicable). Any information about directors, performers or writers you feel is important. Name of network. Call Letters of Local Station (if any), location. broadcast date.

The Hunchback. Based on *The Hunchback of Notre Dame* by Victor Hugo. Perf. Mandy Patankin. TNT. Cable. 16 Mar. 1997.

"Judy Garland: Beyond the Rainbow." *Biography*. A&E cable network. 23 Mar. 1997.

Prose, Francine. Interview with Leonard Lopate. New York & Co. WNYC, New York. 13 Mar. 1997.

Sound Recordings—Music and Spoken Word

When you are citing a recording, start the citation with the person to whom you want to give emphasis. If it is the writer or lyricist, use that as the first name. If you want to note the singer, narrator or engineer, that is fine as well. Note: You do not need to note the media if the sound recording is a CD.

Author or Performer(if available), Last Name, First Name. *Title of Recording*. Date of recording. Additional performer or writer information (optional). Type of medium. Manufacturer, year of issue.

Warren, Harry, writer. *42nd Street: Original Broadway Cast Recording*. Lyrics by Dubin. Perf. Jerry Orbach, Tammy Grimes. LP. RCA Red Seal, 1980.

Shakespeare, William. *All's Well That Ends Well*. Perf.. Dame Edith Evans, Vanessa Redgrave. LP. Living Shakespeare, Inc., 1962.

Khan, Nusrat Fateh Ali and Michael Brooks.
 Night Song. Real World Records, 1995.

If you want to cite one song from a recording, include it (in quotations) before the title of the whole album. The title of a musical composition does not need to be enclosed in quotation marks if it is identified by number and key (Symphony no. 4 in B flat, for example).

Bach, Johann Sebastian. Brandenburg Concer-
. tos no. 4 in G, no. 5 in D and no. 6 in B flat. English Chamber Orchestra. Cond. Leppard, Raymond. Rec. Nov. 1974. Philips, 1975.

Mayfield, Curtis. "New World Order." By Curtis Mayfield, Brian Fleming and Raimundo Thomas. *New World Order*. Warner Bros., 1996.

Gershwin, George. Piano Concerto in F. Perf. Russell Sherman. Orchestra of St. Lukes Cond. Gunther Shuller. American Artists Series, 1986.

Movies and Videos

Similar to a television or radio show. The following is all the information you need, but if you want to add pertinent information about performers or writers, put it between the director and distributor information.

Title of Movie. Dir. Distributor, Year.

Citizen Kane. Dir. Orson Welles. Perf. Orson Welles, Joseph Cotton. Mercury, RKO, 1941.

The Crying Game. Dir. Neil Jordan. Perf. Stephen Rea, Miranda Richardson, Forest Whitaker. Miramax, 1992.

The Manchurian Candidate. Dir. John
Frankenheimer. Perf. Frank Sinatra,
Laurence Harvey. United Artists, 1962.

It may be appropriate to begin with the name of the person whose work you are citing. If the paper or citation is about John Wayne, for example, this entry would be fine:

Wayne, John, perf. *The Man Who Shot Liberty
Valance.* Dir. John Ford. Perf. James
Stewart, John Wayne. Paramount, 1962.

If the citation is a video or filmstrip, include the original release date, if you have it, and the medium and the distributor's name.

Our Literary Heritage. Filmstrips with cassette
and manual. By George and Suzanne
Russell. Educational Filmstrips, Inc., 1970.

Entrepreneurship in Action. Filmstrips and
cassette. Written by R.W. Huff. Nelson
Canada, 1988

Cooperative and Student Team Learning. Video-
cassette. Proj. dir. Gordon H. Felton. NEA
Video Library Series. NEA Professional
Library, 1989.

Troisi, Massimo, actor. *Il Postino* [The Postman].
Videocassette. Dir. Michael Radford.
1995. Miramax, 1997.

Paintings, Sculptures, and Various Works of Art

If you need to cite a work of art, all you need is:

Artist Last Name, First Name. *Title of the Piece.*
Date of Piece (optional). Where the Piece
is located.

DaVinci, Leonardo. *Mona Lisa* [La Jaconde].
Louvre, Paris.

Botticelli. *The Rites of Spring* [La Primavera].
The Uffizzi, Florence.

If the reference is of a picture of the work, include after all the above information the title and publishing information of your source for the picture.

Seurat, Georges. *Gray Weather, Grande Jatte.*
Wildenstein and Co., New York. *The Annenberg Collection.* By Colin B. Bailey, Joseph J. Rishel and Mark Rosenthal. Philadelphia: Philadelphia Museum of Art, 1989.

Miscellaneous Forms

Here are some examples of miscellaneous bibliographic forms for things like cartoons, speeches, and letters.

Agee, Jon. Cartoon. *The New Yorker* 7 Apr. 1997: 49.

Adams, Scott. "Dilbert." Cartoon. *Newsday* [Long Island, New York] 31 Mar. 1997: B17.

Clinton, Bill. Inaugural Address. Washington, DC. 20 Jan. 1997.

Rushdie, Salman. Letter to the author. 6 Dec. 1996.

Browning, Elizabeth Barrett. Letter to Robert Browning. 20 June 1859. Wellesley College Archives. Margaret Clapp Library, Wellesley, Mass.

Case, Steve. Email to the author. 14 Sept. 1995.

Fredericks, Pauline. Memo to Employees, Fredericks Corp. Portland, ME. 28 Feb. 1992.

ELECTRONIC MEDIA

CD-ROMs, Magnetic Tapes, Diskettes

These information sources have become immensely appealing, since so much information can be found in one spot. How do you cite them? There are a few pieces of information that you need to consider. Information is written by one group, perhaps previously published, and then packaged and sold by yet another—the vendor. All these pieces become important, especially if you consider that the same piece of information may show up in several different places. In the name of clarity, you need to let you reader know exactly which version you are citing.

Periodical Databases

If the material is from a CD-ROM that is issued periodically (such as those you may find in your library) and is a compilation of information that you may have found in print, use the following format:

> Author Last Name, First Name. "Title of Piece." *Original Source* original date, edition: original section and page. *Title of Database*. Type of Medium. Vendor. Date of Database Publication.

> Marie, Annette. "A Theory on Adolescent Literacy." U.S., *Educational Resources Information Center*, 1994. *ERIC*. CD-ROM. Silverplatter. May 1994.

If you cannot find the name of the vendor or the date of the CD-ROM or diskette's release, include as much information as you have. If no original source is referenced (some material is published directly on CD-ROM or disk) just use the date of the piece.

Nonperiodical Databases

If the CD-ROM or disk is not one that is issued and updated regularly (weekly, monthly, yearly), use this as your citation:

Author (if available). "Title of the Piece." *Title of the Disk*. Release, Version or Edition. Type of Media. City of Publication: Vendor, date.

"Bosnia and Herzegovina." *The New Grolier Multimedia Encyclopedia*. Rel. 6. CD-ROM. n.p. Online Computer Systems, Inc., 1993.

"Map of Bosnia." *The Software Toolworks World Atlas*. Ver. 4. CD-ROM. Novato: The Software Toolworks, 1991–1993.

"Wesleyan University." *Peterson's College Database*. Magnetic Tape. Princeton: Peterson's, 1995.

The Constitution Notebook. Ver. 3.4. Computer disk, booklet. TCNbP Company, 1989-1996.

Robinson, Randal and Peter Holben Weir. *Shakespeare's Language*. Computer disk. East Lansing: Instructional Media Center, 199?.

If there is more than one type of electronic media in your package of information (for example a CD-ROM and videotape), just list all the types of media, each separated by a comma.

Online Databases and Services

These citations are similar to those for electronic databases. When you are referencing the medium, use the term "online." The "publisher" is usually the computer service or network through which you accessed the information. Because databases change so frequently, always be sure to note the date of access. Sometimes you are accessing information that was previously printed elsewhere. Make a note if the material was published previously. Here's the general format:

Author Last Name, First Name. "Title of Piece."
Original Source. Original Source date,
original source edition: original source
pages (if applicable). Title of Electronic
Source. Online. Information Provider.
Date of Access.

Evan, Tracy. "International Relations: For-
eign." *Compton's Living Encyclopedia.*
Compton's Learning Company, 1996.
Online. America Online. 10 June 1996.

"Nobel Prize Winners in Peace." *Compton's
Living Encyclopedia.* Compton's Learning
Company, 1996. Online. America Online.
10 June 1996.

INTERNET SOURCES

Internet sources, World Wide Web pages, FTP and Gopher sites,
and Newsgroups have unusual characteristics. Here are a few
things to keep in mind.

The "author" may be listed as an e-mail address. She may
simply have a title such as "webmaster" or "maintainer." If you
do not have at least an email address, treat the author as you
would a corporate author, citing the author as the organization
or company that runs the page. Make sure you examine all the
links from the page thoroughly to be sure no author is listed.

Although it is still considered optional, most professors want
you to supply the Internet address (the URL) for the document
you are citing. This allows them to verify information. We will
give examples for several different types of information you
may be citing from the Internet.

Ejournal

An *Ejournal,* or *electronic journal,* is an academic journal published online. Some have print counterparts, others do not. To
reference an article found in an ejournal:

Author Last name, First name. "Title of the Article." *Name of Ejournal* volume and number information (Date of Ejournal): number of pages or n.pag. if no pagination is supplied. Online. Network. Date of Access. Available URL (optional).

Burrows, J.F. "Numbering the Streaks of the Tulip? Reflections on a Challenge to the Use of Statistical Methods in Computational Stylistics." *CH Working Papers* A.2 (Feb. 1992): n.pag. Online. Internet. 11 Nov. 1996. Available www.chass.utoronto.ca:8080/epc/chwp/titles.html#Articles.

Trombley, William. "UC Regents: Lots of Pomp, Little Circumstance." *Crosstalk* 3.2 (Sept. 1995): n.pag. Online. Internet. 1 Dec. 1996.

Online Version of a Newspaper or Magazine

Quite a number of newspapers and magazines are publishing online versions. Some of them have extensive archives and allow searching on the Internet to be as easy as searching the microfiche in the library. Here's the format for an article you're citing that has been previously published:

Author Last Name, First Name. "Title of Article." *Original Source Title* Original Source Date: Original Source section and page numbers. Online Source Name. Online. Network. Date of Access. Available URL (optional).

Phillips, Natalie. "Tort-Reform Battle Heats Up in Juneau." *Anchorage Daily News* 23 Mar. 1997: n.pag. *Anchorage Daily News HTML Edition.* Online. Internet. 23 Mar. 1997. Available www.adn.com.

Walsh, Mark. "Birds of a Feather Do Deals Together." *Crain's New York Business* 17–23 Mar. 1997: n.pag. *Crain's New York Business Online*. Online. Internet. 1 Apr. 1997.

Online Texts

While you can access many full texts online these days, be sure you are accessing from a reputable institution. Columbia University, the University of Virginia, and Indiana University are just a few of the large universities that are archiving many texts. Most professors will want to see which version of a text you are using, so try to stick to archives that provide this information (publisher, editor, translator for example).

Here's the format:

Author Last Name, First Name. *Title of Text.* Ed. or Trans. if applicable. Original Publishing Place: Original Publisher, Date of Original Publication. Online. Name of Archive. Network. Date of Access. Available URL (optional).

Hobbes, Thomas. *Leviathan, or, The Matter, Forme, and Power of a Common-Wealth, Ecclesiaticall and Civill.* Based on Eds. of 1651 and 1839. Pittsboro, N.C.: InteLex Corp., 1994? Online. Columbia University Digital Lib. Collec. Internet. 31 Mar. Available www.columbia.edu/cu/libraries/digital/texts/pastmasters.html.

Original Online Material

Not everything online has been previously published. Try to find an author, if possible. While an email address is acceptable, make sure you have tried all links to find a real name. If no name is available, treat the source as having no author. Follow the same basic format, giving URL and date of access.

Rebello, Rodrigo. "History of Mozart." *W.A. Mozart's Page.* Online. Internet. 7 Feb. 1997. Available: http://www.geocities.com/Vienna/5314/eindex.html

Citing Your Sources in the Text

Now that you have finished your bibliography or list of works cited, you need to complete your documentation for the footnotes, endnotes, or embedded citations. What type of citation should you use? Most of the time that is dictated by the professor. MLA style uses embedded citations and most professors favor it. Ask your professor which is the preferred method for your paper.

Footnotes, Endnotes, and Embedded Citations

What are the differences among these three types of citation?

Footnotes make reference to the document at the bottom (or foot) of the page. While in the old days of typewriters (gasp!) this meant calculating how much space to leave at the bottom of the page—depending on the number of citations per page—now your word processor does all that for you. A footnote is referenced in the text by a number.

Endnotes are just like footnotes, except all the documentation is at the end of the paper, not at the foot of each page. Most professors prefer footnotes to endnotes, but always ask. A footnote or endnote looks like this:

> From 1543 through the eighteenth century, water in England gained importance for agriculture and transportation.[1]

Either at the bottom of the page (if it is a footnote) or at the end of your report (if it is an endnote), you will see the corresponding citation:

> [2] Romain L. Klaasen, "Brief History of Real Estate Appraisal and Organizations," *The Appraisal Journal,* vol. 44 (July 1976), p. 378.

Embedded citations are probably the easiest for students. The citation is not referred to, but simply follows the information you are referencing, in parentheses. The above reference would look like this:

> From 1543 through the 18th century, water in England gained importance for agriculture and transportation (Klassen 378).

Now, let's review the rules for citations. We will cover embedded citations first, as they are preferred and simplest.

Embedded Citations

Embedded citations (used in MLA style) are nice and simple: No messy op.cits. or ibids. In the embedded citation, instead of a raised number, just follow the area where you wish to make your citation with a parenthetical reference. Use whatever you began your bibliographic reference with as the reference for the citation. If you have an author, use the author's last name. If the author was unknown and you used the title, use a shortened form of that for the citation.

The idea of parenthetical references is to keep the flow of the paper as smooth as possible. If you have mentioned the author and referenced the work in your writing, you do not need a citation unless you are referring to a specific section. For example "Mill's utilitarian philosophy was well known." would not need a citation to Mill's *Utilitarianism*. If you have mentioned the author in the quote or paraphrase, you need only make reference to the page to which you are referring. Sometimes there is no specific page reference—you may be summarizing and therefore referring to a whole document or section. In that case, you need only put the author's name.

> Lomax tells us that over thirty such organizations exist (30).

> Some of the new programs Bleier mentions that are administered are the PEN/Faulkner award for fiction, summer institutes for junior and senior high school teachers, and noon-time free concerts (45).

If you have not mentioned the author in your comment, the name must be included in the embedded citation.

These materials must be requested one piece at a time, used in the open reading rooms, and returned at the end of the day (Dalrymple and Goodrum 19).

The message was brought forth by a new messenger (Finch 34).

Use the same form if you are referring to an author.

While this may be true, Kierkegaard felt that this would never be proved (39).

While this may be true, some felt that it would never be proved (Kierkegaard 39).

If the reference is a quotation, place the citation outside the quotation marks, with punctuation afterwards. If the reference is a long quotation that is set in from the text, place the citation, after the quotation mark, before any other puncuation.

Stern felt that rare books can be "a link with the past, yet . . . marvelously current and contemporary" (427).

If the quote is set off from the text, put the page reference with the quote, after the period and followed by a period:

If the reference is to a multivolume work, cite the volume number, followed by colon and page number. For example:

The reason Bradley felt it was true was clear to all around him (6:456).

After all his hard work was finished, Kissinger went into private practice (Phelps 5:67).

Works Listed by Title

Use the same format if you are citing works given by title. If the title is mentioned in the text, you only need to note a page number if applicable. If not, give a shortened version of the title (unless it is short already) and the page number. Always use the first main word in your entry when you shorten, so that your reader will know where to look in your bibliography.

That idea was popular even as far back as the nineteenth century (*Annals* 5:67).

We can read in volume five of *Annals of America* that this was true (67).

In *Annals of America*, we can read that this was true (5:67).

Two or More Works by the Same Author

If you have two or more works by the same author, obviously the author name alone will not be sufficient. Use the author name, followed by a comma, a shortened version of the title and the page reference. For example:

We could see that he was no longer able to play at that point (Winthrop, *Farewell* 55)

As before, if you make reference to the author, title or both in the text, you may leave those parts out of the citation.

Reference to a Reference

Sometimes you get information from a collection or anthology. If, for example, you are referencing a speech reprinted in an anthology, use the abbreviation *qtd. in*, for *quoted in*, and then your citation.

It was then that Lilienthal, in his confirmation hearings for head of the Atomic Energy Commission, said that "[his] convictions are not so much concerned with what [he is] against as what [he is] for; and that excludes a lot of things automatically" (qtd. in Ravitch 295).

Classic Books, Plays, and Poems

If you are citing a work that may be available in several editions, you may want to give more information, say, chapter, verse, or scene references. Put any additional information you feel is necessary after a semicolon after the page number.

The reference in *Moby Dick* was clear. (Melville 7; ch. 1).

More Than One Reference

If you need to refer to more than one work from your bibliography, just separate references by a semicolon. Follow all the rules from before.

> Several works have substantiated that theory
> (Williams 67; Smith 7; Julia 6:78).

Avoid making your references so long that they interrupt the text. If you find yourself citing so much in the parentheses that you are taking up a line or more with your citation, you should rethink your text and break it up so that you may reference things separately.

Scientific Citation

In pure scientific citation, you will probably be expected to cite the date after the author name. Page numbers may not even be required. In science, the date of the work you are using is really more important than the page number. Ask your professor if you are unsure, but in the absence of instructions, use dates only in scientific citation. For example:

> The mitochondria were found to tumble rather
> than scoot towards the pathogen (Smith 1996).

FOOTNOTES AND ENDNOTES

When you are writing any kind of citation, you are simply letting the reader know which of the works in your bibliography you are citing, and where in the work you found this particular bit of information. Remember, you need to cite any work you use that is not your own, even if it is simply a paraphrase. If you're using Chicago rather than MLA style, you will use footnotes or endnotes instead of embedded citations. Let's take an example to illustrate the basic idea. Say you use the book *Ecology and the Politics of Scarcity* by William Ophuls. Your bibliography would have the following entry:

> Ophuls, William. *Ecology and the Politics of
> Scarcity*. San Francisco: W.H. Freeman
> and Company, 1977.

A passage on page 100 in the book reads:

"In sum, geothermal power has a significant potential, but only extreme optimists foresee this form of energy constituting more than 20 percent of supply."

And in your paper, you use the line:

Even though geothermal power has the possibility of being a significant energy source, most feel that it could not be more than 20 percent.[1]

You need to follow it with a citation. If this is the first note in your paper, use the number one, raised up one half line from the text:

[1] William Ophuls, *Ecology and the Politics of Scarcity* (San Francisco: W.H. Freeman and Company, 1977), 100.

What is the difference between a footnote and a bibliographic entry? First of all, there are commas, rather than periods following the author name and the title of the work. The author name is not reversed, as in a bibliographic entry. The publishing information is enclosed in parentheses, and followed by a page reference.

Let's run through the following bibliographic entries from the previous section to see how they would look as footnotes or endnotes.

Jahoda, Gloria. *The Trail of Tears: The Story of the American Indian Removal 1813-1855.* New York: Holt, Rinehardt and Winston, 1975.

[1] Gloria Jahoda, *The Trail of Tears: The Story of the American Indian Removal 1813-1855* (New York: Holt Rinehardt), 1975 50.

Thoms, W.J., ed. *A Collection of Early English Prose Romances.* London: Pickering, 1858.

[2] W.J. Thoms, ed., *A Collection of Early English Prose Romances* (London: Pickering, 1858), 212.

X, Malcolm, with Alex Haley. *The Autobiography of Malcolm X*. New York: Grove, 1964.

[3]Malcolm X with Alex Haley, *The Autobiography of Malcolm X* (New York: Grove, 1964), 78.

American Bar Association. *A Portable Guide to Federal Conspiracy Law: Developing Strategies for Criminal and Civil Cases*. Chicago: PPM of the American Bar Association, 1997.

[4]American Bar Association, *A Portable Guide to Federal Conspiracy Law: Developing Strategies for Criminal and Civil Cases* (Chicago: PPM of the American Bar Association, 1977), 3.

Camus, Albert. "The Myth of Sisyphus." *The Myth of Sisyphus and Other Essays*. Trans. Justin O'Brien. New York: Knopf, 1955. 54–55.

[5]Albert Camus, "The Myth of Sisyphus." *The Myth of Sisyphus and Other Essays*, trans. Justin O'Brien (New York: Knopf, 1955), 54.

Bradley, James. "Bowery Savings Bank." *The Encyclopedia of New York City*. Ed. Kenneth T. Jackson. New Haven: Yale University Press: New York: The New-York Historical Society, 1995.

[6]James Bradley, "Bowery Savings Bank," *The Enclyclopedia of New York City*, ed. Kenneth T. Jackson (New Haven: Yale University Press: New York: The New York Historical Society, 1995) 132.

Matthews, John. Foreword. *The Encyclopedia of Arthurian Legends*. By Ronan Coghlan. Shaftesbury, Dorset: Element, 1991. iii–iv.

[7] John Matthews, foreword, *The Ency-clopedia of Arthurian Legends*, by Ronan Coghlan (Shaftesbury, Dorset: Element, 1991), p iii.

"Confessions of an Erstwhile Child." *The New Republic.* 15 June 1974: p 11.

[8]"Confessions of an Erstwhile Child," *The New Republic*, 15 June 1974: 11.

Bryden, M.P. "Attentional Strategies and Short-Term Memory in Dichotic Listening." *Cognitive Psychology* 2 (1971): 99–116.

[9]M.P Bryden, "Attentional Strategies and Short-Term Memory in Dichotic Listening," *Cognitive Psychology* 2 (1971): 99–116.

Eichenwald, Kurt. "U.S. Expands Search of Columbia/HCA in Texas." *New York Times* 21 Mar. 1997: D1+.

[10]Kurt Eichenwald, "U.S. Expands Search of Columbia / HCA in Texas," *New York Times* 21 Mar. 1997: D1+.

Blumenthal, Sidney. "The Cold War and the Closet." Rev. of *Whittaker Chambers*, by Sam Tanenhaus. *The New Yorker* 17 Mar. 1997: 112–117.

[11]Sidney Blumenthal, "The Cold War and the Closet," rev. of *Whittaker Chambers*, by Sam Tanenhaus, *The New Yorker* 17 Mar. 1997: 114.

"Judy Garland: Beyond the Rainbow." *Biography.* A&E cable network. 23 Mar. 1997.

[12]"Judy Garland: Beyond the Rainbow," *Biography*, A&E cable network: 23 Mar. 1997.

Shakespeare, William. *All's Well That Ends Well.* Perf. Dame Edith Evans, Vanessa Redgrave. LP. Living Shakespeare, Inc., 1962.

[13]William Shakespeare, *All's Well That Ends Well*, Perf. Dame Edith Evans, Vanessa Redgrave, LP, Living Shakespeare, Inc., 1962.

Citizen Kane. Dir. Orson Welles. Perf. Orson Welles, Joseph Cotton. Mercury, RKO, 1941.

[14]*Citizen Kane*, dir. Orson Welles, perf. Orson Welles, Joseph Cotton, Mercury, RKO, 1941.

Cooperative and Student Team Learning. Videocassette. proj. dir. Gordon H. Felton. NEA Video Library Series. NEA Professional Library, 1989.

[15]*Cooperative and Student Team Learning*, Videocassette. proj. dir. Gordon H. Felton, NEA Video Library Series, NEA Professional Library, 1989.

"Bosnia and Herzegovina." *The New Grolier Multimedia Encyclopedia*. Rel. 6. CD-ROM. Online Computer Systems, Inc., 1993.

[16]"Bosnia and Herzegovina," *The New Grolier Multimedia Encyclopedia*, rel. 6, CD-ROM (Online Computer Systems, Inc., 1993).

Trombley, William. "UC Regents: Lots of Pomp, Little Circumstance." *Crosstalk* 3.2 (Sept. 1995): n.pag. Online. Internet. 1 Dec. 1996.

[17]William Trombley, "UC Regents: Lots of Pomp, Little Circumstance," *Crosstalk* 3.2 (Sept. 1995): n.pag, online, Internet, 1 Dec. 1996.

Walsh, Mark. "Birds of a Feather Do Deals Together." *Crain's New York Business* 17–23 Mar. 1997: n.pag. *Crain's New York Business Online*. Online. Internet. 1 Apr. 1997.

[18]Mark Walsh, "Birds of a Feather Do Deals Together," *Crain's New York Business*, 17–23 Mar. 1997:n.pag., *Crain's New York Business Online*, online, Internet, 1 Apr. 1997.

Hobbes, Thomas. *Leviathan, or, The Matter, Forme, and Power of a Common-Wealth, Ecclesiaticall and Civill.* Based on Eds. of 1651 and 1839. Pittsboro, N.C.: InteLex Corp., 1994? Online. Columbia University Digital Lib. Collec. Internet. 31 Mar. Available www.columbia.edu/cu/libraries/digital/texts/pastmasters.html.

[19]Thomas Hobbes, *Leviathan, or, The Matter, Forme, and Power of a Common-Wealth, Ecclesiaticall and Civill,* based on Eds. of 1651 and 1839 (Pittsboro, N.C.: InteLex Corp., 1994?) online, Columbia University Digital Lib. Collec., Internet, 31 Mar. 1997, available www.columbia.edu/cu/libraries/digital/texts/pastmasters.html.

REPEATED REFERENCES TO THE SAME WORK

If you are citing the same work, you do not need to write out the full citation again. MLA rules allow you to simply use the author's last name and page reference (just like the information given in an embedded citation). If you have two or more works by the same author, use a shortened version of the title with the author name.

[4]Helms 56.

[5]Helms, *Fearless* 67.

Ibid., Op Cit. and Loc. Cit.

Many professors will prefer you use the abbreviations above if you are citing the same source more than once. Here they are with their full Latin terms (in case you're ever on *Jeopardy*):

- Ibid. (*ibidem*)— meaning "in the same place."

- Op. cit. (*opere citato*)—"in the work cited."

- Loc. cit. (*loco citato*)—"in the place cited."

Here is a sample of a section of footnotes using the above abbreviations.

[1]Stephen Knight, *Form and Ideology in Crime Fiction* (Bloomington, Indiana: Indiana University Press, 1980) 45.

[2]Ibid., 55.

[3]Dilys Winn, *Murder Ink: The Mystery Reader's Companion* (New York: Workman Publishing, 1977), 44.

[4]Knight, op. cit., 77.

[5]Betty Rosenberg, *Genreflecting: A Guide to Reading Interests in Genre Fiction* (Littleton, Colorado: Libraries, Unlimited, 1982) 143.

[6]Loc. cit.

[7]Ibid., 49.

[8]Winn, op. cit., p. 66

Explanations

1. This is the first footnote reference for the book *Form and Ideology in Crime Fiction* by Stephen Knight. The writer is referencing material used on page 45.

2. This is a reference to the same book as the previous note, Knight's *Form and Ideology in Crime Fiction*, but for a different page, page 55.

3. The first reference to the book by Dilys Winn, *Murder Ink: The Mystery Reader's Companion*; the note refers to material on page 44.

4. This refers back to the Knight book referenced in note 1, for page 77.

5. This is the first reference to a third source, Rosenberg's *Genreflecting: A Guide to Reading in Genre Fiction*, page 143.

6. Loc. cit. refers to the Rosenberg work in the previous note: same book, same page.

7. Ibid. refers to the previous note as well— the Rosenberg book—but a different page, page 49.

8. This refers back to the Winn book, page 66.

(Note: These terms are generally no longer recommended by the MLA, so be sure to check with your professor before using them.)

Forms Of Footnotes And Endnotes

As you can see from the examples above, it is relatively easy to transform a bibliographic entry into a footnote or endnote. We recommend using the "copy" and "paste" functions on your word-processing program: Copy the bibliographic entry exactly, so that you have the information correct, and then make the adjustments necessary to turn it into a footnote. Be sure to add your page reference.

If you are using footnotes, you have the option of numbering them consecutively throughout your document or numbering them starting at number one for each page. If you are typing, it is probably easier to number starting at one for each new page. However, if you are using a word-processing program that does footnotes for you, it will automatically number consecutively throughout the document.

The number should always follow the information you are citing—don't put it in the middle of a sentence or before the punctuation. There are no spaces between the period and the footnote. The footnote number is not followed by a period.

Correct

The claim was fostered by the notion that the allegations were false.[1]

Incorrect

> The claim was foster by the notion[1] that the allegations were false.

Single-space within the footnote and double-space between footnotes. The notation at the bottom of the page should be indented five spaces on the first line, and taken to the margin after. The footnote numeral in the citation, like its reference on the page is raised one half line (superscript) and not followed by a period.

Correct

> [1]Lynn E. Birge, *Serving Adult Learners: A Public Library Tradition* (Chicago: American Library Association, 1981), 97.
>
> [2]Charles H. Busha and Stephen P. Harter, *Research Methods in Librarianship* (San Diego: Academic Press, Inc., 1980), 169.

There should be two lines between the text on the page and the footnote section. Again, if you are using a footnote function on your word processor, they will be inserted automatically. If you are typing, you need to figure about how many footnotes will be on the bottom of each pages you type and allow about an inch for each footnote. Since you have an inch margin at the foot of the page, if you plan to have three footnotes on a page, you need to allow four inches at the bottom after your text. Type a line between the text and the footnotes.

If you are using endnotes, you will number them consecutively throughout the document and immediately following the text, you will label a new page NOTES in all capitals, centered on the page, 1 inch from the top. Endnotes should be double-spaced, similarly to your bibliography. Unlike footnotes, the number that references the note is not raised: Indent the first line five spaces in from the margin, followed by a period, two spaces and then the citation.

Content Notes

Footnotes and endnotes may also be used to add content to your paper. Number a content footnote just as you would a reference footnote—in chronological order with the other footnotes. A content footnote is used to explain or comment on the information you have just presented, to present something to the reader as an aside to give some emphasis to what you have already said, or to refer to a table, graph or piece of information that comes at a different point in the report. Some examples of content footnotes:

[1]This particular incident was later dramatized in the Truman Capote novel *In Cold Blood*.

[2]The author acknowledges the assistance of the research department in this cause.

[3]Please refer to table A in the addendum.

[4]While the case was never solved, there was much speculation on the part of the police department that Jones was guilty.

If you are using endnotes, you may wish to indicate content footnotes on the same page as the text you are commenting on. If this is the case, use the asterisk (*) to indicate a content footnote at the bottom of the page.

5

The Final Draft

Give us the tools and we will finish the job.

—Winston Churchill

Now that all your hard work is really done, you can settle into the fun part (at least in our opinion): preparing your final draft. Although the rules for how your paper should be presented will not vary whether you are working on a computer or a typewriter, your job will be much easier if you can use a computer. The word-processing program was designed to make the task of editing, correcting, formatting, and printing a paper as easy as possible. Since most schools and libraries have computers for their patrons to use, we feel that just about anyone should be able to avail herself of this great time-saver.

Whether your rough draft is on a computer or on loose-leaf paper, now is the time for you to do a detailed read-through. Make sure you have properly credited all your sources. Make sure your ideas flow from beginning to end, and that they have been fully expressed and supported. There are two really good techniques to double-check all of the parts of your paper.

If you are working on a computer, print out a copy of your paper. It's a good idea to get a feel for how your paper looks.

Many students find it difficult to determine whether the structure of the paper is clear until they are able to see the actual printed document.

Read it out loud. That's right—out loud. It can be of great help to actually hear your words. A well-written paper will sound good. Sometimes you can't get a feel for that by reading it to yourself. Reading your paper out loud is also enormously helpful in getting you to edit your sentences and paragraphs. Let your ear guide you as to what sounds best.

Ask someone else to read through the paper for you. This is especially important if you're working on a long research paper over a long period of time. You may find that you can't really separate yourself enough from the subject to make an objective assessment of the job you've done. Frequently, you've done so much reading that you lose sight of the fact that your reader may not know as much as you do. Remember, always consider your audience. If you are writing for an educated reader, ask a fellow classmate to read through your paper. If you are writing for a general audience, it would probably be most helpful to ask a friend who has very little background in your subject.

You should make any notes and edits on your rough draft, so that as you prepare to write the final copy, you will have all of the information in front of you. Review the grammar sections, make sure that the style is appropriate and clear. Now we are ready to get into the nuts and bolts of how your paper should look. We are going to use standard guidelines for the physical requirements of a paper, but always check with your professor, who may have specific instructions. In the absence of contrary advice, these guidelines will be acceptable.

PAPER

You should always use standard $8\frac{1}{2}$ x 11-inch white or cream-colored paper. Do not fool around with unusual-colored paper; it will only detract your reader from the content of your paper, and it may actually lower your grade. Always use a good quality paper. A twenty-pound bond is acceptable. If you are writing a thesis, you may want to use a twenty-pound rag content paper. Paper that is too thin will tear easily. Erasable paper, while very convenient if you are typing, smudges too easily.

FONTS

Don't use silly fonts. While you may think that writing your whole paper in a script font may look great, most of your professors will not agree. Use a standard font, like Times New Roman, in a 12-point size. Using large or silly fonts will also distract your reader.

Make sure you have a good cartridge in your printer, or a good ribbon in your typewriter. Use a high-quality ink-jet or laser printer, if possible. If you have a lower quality daisy wheel printer, for example, consider printing out your report on another printer. The paper should be printed or typed in black or dark-blue ink so that it is easy to read. You may be allowed to submit a handwritten paper (especially if it is a short assignment). The same basic rules apply. Your writing should be legible, not too large or too small, and written in black or blue ink only. Most teachers will insist that lengthy research papers (anything more than a few pages) be typewritten. Write, type or print your report on one side of the paper only. Never use both sides of the paper.

SPACING

A paper should always be double-spaced throughout. This includes the endnotes and bibliography, header and title. If you are submitting a handwritten paper, you should only write on every other line. Footnotes should be single-spaced within the notes and double-spaced between notes.

MARGINS

If you are putting your paper in a binder, your margins should be one and a half inches in from the left side (to accommodate the binder) and one inch in from all other sides. If you don't use a binder, make all margins one inch in from the side. Make sure to ask your teacher if a binder is required or even allowed. Many teachers do not like papers submitted in binders, as they may be more difficult to read if the binder does not allow the pages to lie flat. Other professors will insist that the paper is handed in bound. In the absence of instruction, use a paper clip. This method allows the reader to remove the clip to read your paper more easily.

PAGE NUMBERS

Every page should be numbered consecutively, with the exception of a title page, if you have one. Notes, bibliography, and tables are all numbered as part of the paper. The page number should be flush with the right margin and preceded by your name. This is useful in the event that a page of your paper is separated from the rest of the text. The name and page number should be half an inch below the top of the paper. As the text is one inch from the top, the page number will be halfway between the top of the page and the text.

TITLES

You may not need to write a title page. If not, simply start your heading one inch from the top on the first page of the paper, at the left margin. You should include the instructor's name, course number, and date. The title should be double-spaced below the last line of the heading, centered on the page. While you should follow the rules for capitalizing titles, you shouldn't underline or put your title in quotations. Here is a sample of the beginning of a paper:

Anders 1

Pamela Anders
Professor Wilson
Research Methods 210
1 April 1997

The Value of Special Collections in the Library

    While the heart of the library is certainly its circulating book collection, its personality can best be seen in its special collection. At its best, the special collection is a reflection of the unique personality of the community served by the library. The special collection may consist purely of reading materials or it may reach into different media: artwork, computers, objects or even trained counselors. The purpose of this paper is to explore...

If you do want to use a title page, put the title in the center of the page, using the rules for capitalizing titles, double-spacing if more than one line is necessary. Center the title on the page. Put the word *By* four lines below the title, centered as well, and your name centered two lines below that. You should have the professor's name, course number, and date on three separate lines, double-spaced and centered on the bottom of the title page. For example:

The Value of Special Collections in the Library

By
Pamela Anders

Professor Wilson
Research Methods 210
1 April 1997

TABLES, CHARTS, PICTURES, AND THE LIKE

You may have tables or other visual aids in your report. Include them within the body of the text as much as possible. Use your common sense here. While you don't want your reader to have to flip back and forth to reference a table or chart, you also don't want to fill your paper with so much "filler" that there's no room for the text. If you have a series of tables that would interfere with the flow of the text too much, put them in an addendum.

You should double-space tables and any accompanying text or notes, as well as text that accompanies pictures or charts. If you have a picture from another source that you would like to include, just leave the appropriate amount of space on your page, print the page, tape on the picture, and make a copy of the whole thing. This will look much neater. Be sure to copy onto the same type of paper as you are using for the rest of your report.

Label tables consecutively throughout the report: Table 1, Table 2, and so forth. Pictures and graphs may be labeled as Fig. 1, Fig. 2 (for Figure 1, Figure 2) and so forth. In the caption, cite the full footnote reference for the information. For example:

Nobel Peace Prize Winners, 1901-1905

Year	Winner	Life Span	Nationality
1901	Jean H. Dunant	1828–1910	Swiss
1901	Frederic Passy	1822–1912	French
1902	Elie Ducommon	1833–1906	Swiss
1902	Charles A. Gobat	1843–1914	Swiss
1903	Sir William R. Cremer	1838–1908	English
1904	Institute of International Law, Ghent		
1905	Baroness Bertha von Suttner	1843–1914	Austrian

Source: "Nobel Prizewinner in Peace," *Compton's Living Encyclopedia*, Compton's Learning Company, 1996 Online, America Online, 4 June 1996.

CORRECTIONS

With a word-processor program, you should be able to make any corrections to your document and reprint only those pages to which corrections were made. If you are typing, however, you may make minor corrections directly onto a typewritten page. Use dark blue or black ink and make a neat insertion with a caret,^, directly above the line. If you have more than two or three such corrections to make, you are probably better off re-typing the page.

Use spell checkers with caution; forget grammar checkers. Remember that spell checkers will not pick up words that are spelled correctly but used incorrectly. Grammar checking programs are simply useless at this stage. Careful proofreading is the best way to be sure that your paper is well written and error free.

AND THUS . . .

Research papers aren't so terrible; they just call for a concerted plan of attack and some scheduling. If you ever get stuck and don't know what to write next, ask yourself, "What am I trying to say?" and write that down. That is the surest way to clear, direct communication through writing.

Appendix

EDITING DRILL FOR THE RESEARCH PAPER

Edit this five-page paper, paying attention to the editing guidelines in chapter four. We mean it; we actually want you to write in the book. Get a red pen and go. Then compare with the edits in the section following this paper.

Candy Bars and Psychology

Psychology has long posited a connection between the psyche and taste in food. The noted professor of food and psychology, Ima Hogg, says, "While many attempt to discover the secrets of the mind through outmoded techniques of psychoanalysis and clinical psychology, the true frontier on which we are discovering the key to personality is by assessing what people eat. Beyond this we cannot hope to go further." (WRITE IN FOOTNOTE FOR HOGG'S STUDY) Hogg's studies relating diet and psychosis went on for over twenty-five years, and they clearly show what any reasonable person has long suspected: you are what you eat. Think of the current fad of liquid diet shakes, so appropriate to our American society, caught between the Calvinist puritanism of our history and the relentless greed and self-indulgence of our current market economy. Consider President Clinton and his fondness for fast food, the food of a person of action, someone ready to lead! Or remember the self-destructive habits of the romans, fulfilling the slightest desire with loads of tempting delicacies, then running off to the vomitoria to rid themselves and begin again. This demonstrates a clear connection between what one eats and who one is. And indeed, the existence of a connection between food and personality points to the likelihood of a connection between candy bar choice and personality disorder.

Many studies have been done to test this theory and the results of them are here.

Much has been written about those candy bars that combine the various candy elements: nougat, caramel, nuts. The desire for all the things at once, the inability to make any sort of a concrete choice is typical of the boy/man who suffers from the peter pan syndrome, and the combination bar is his candy of choice. This is evidenced on grounds both academic and emotional. In her ground-breaking treatise on the subject, Dr. Lotta Kaloreese interviewed a group of 2,500 male participants between the ages of 23 and 55. Of those who said they were either involved or willing to be involved in what they themselves termed a mature lifestyle, only 19.7% indicated the combination bar, or "Snickers," as their primary candy choice. Of those who professed a longing to return to childhood, or to remain a child indefinitely, an astonishing 78% indicated a strong preference for the Snickers bar as their primary candy choice. (CITE KALOREESE'S STUDY) Numerical results this overwhelming cannot be ignored: Snickers is the bar of those who would be children forever.

Another stunning example is the historical references of the caramel. One of the most traditional forms of confection, the caramel is the choice of those who are overly sentimental and prone to emotional outbursts and flights of fancy. Many soft-hearted artists have long called the caramel their favorite, with laudatory remarks often taking the form of song and poetry. "Boy, there's nothing a like better than a chocolate bar with caramel in it." (CHECK MLA, DO I NEED TO FOOTNOTE THIS IF I HAVE HIS NAME?) says Barry Manilow, renowned emotional person. This sort of confession is seen over and over again in memoirs of emotional people. In writings by John Denver, Sally Field, Tchaikovsky, and other softies one can find multiple references to caramel. This happens too frequently to be mere happenstance, one has yet another reason to believe that there must be some connection between the form of candy sugar takes, and the type of person who wants that candy.

Yet another example is apparent in the strong connection between nut bars and those who love them, the tough guys both male and female. While much has been written on the connection between nuts of all types and risk-taking daredevils, including the tie between skydiving and various types of nut brittle, the clearest delineation of candy to personality is peanuts to machismo. The study was done is most particularly seen in the desire of river guides, hunters, and rock climbers for Mr. Goodbar, the peanut chocolate bar. (RICH) Dr. Rich performed his study over two years in all the venues mentioned. He used three groups among each participants. To the first group he offered a buffet table at the end of their trips which contained fruit, chocolate bars of assorted types other than Mr. Goodbars, arranged with the Mr. Goodbars at the back less reachable part of the table, with the fruit and other candy toward the front. The participants—94% of them—reached to the back to get their Mr. Goodbars. Several, 62% of those who chose the Mr. Goodbar, were heard to grunt the word "Good." Upon taking the bar. Dr. Rich considered the possibility that these participants had chosen the bars because they were at the back and therefore more difficult to reach and therefore a greater "prize" to these rough and tumble participants, and to try to weed these out he set up another buffet at which the Mr. Goodbars were set near the front in easy reach, no challenge at all. Again an overwhelming majority, 86% this time, chose the Mr. Goodbar over any other candy. His final group was served with a mixed buffet on which the candy was arranged every which way, with the results the same. This buffet was, in fact, picked clean of all peanut related candy, with fruit and other candy left strewn apart, due, he hypothesizes, to the desire of "macho" individuals for a hunt for their prey. On returning to his University to organize and publish his findings he tried a control group, and offered an audience of 2,000 anthropology students the same buffet. Only an astonishing 21% chose the Mr. Goodbar, and the candy proportions were the same. There can be no clearer evidence than this that there is indeed, a correlation between candy type and personality.

Scientific reason would lead one to consider whether this applied to only the nut bar, or the caramel. Recent research in the chocolate bar field has uncovered some startling findings. People who purchase the plain chocolate and milk chocolate bars generally complain of a feeling of a life left unfulfilled, of feelings and possibilities left unexplored. (WHOEVER) Similar studies of randomly selected buyers of toffee bars, including the Heath and the Skor bar indicate that these buyers, or at least 89% of these buyers, can be classified as suffering from superiority complexes, defined as the strong belief that they are better than the rest of us. The compelling evidence linking the lover of coconut bars and the psychopath only cements the bond.

There are many in both the scientific and confectionery community who protest that chocolate bar preference is merely a matter of personal taste, and hence unrelated to any personality quirks. Most notable among these groups are Dr. Faust and Dr. Pheelgud. Dr. Faust notes that much as the experiments have done to set up control groups, the studies done have not covered a wide enough expanse of the population. FOOTNOTE? OR LATER ON? In fact, all the studies, he notes, have been done in the United States where the candy bars advertise their images via television commercials. Thus it is these media images of the bars that people respond to, not the bars themselves. Dr. Pheelgud notes in his book, Candy Bars and Personality: There's No Connection, that candy bars and what goes in them changes over time, for instance licorice is not nearly as popular as it was in the early forties. PHEELGUD This change over time indicates to her that there is no real correlation, because that would indicate a change in human personality type within the space of a decade, and this she considers unlikely.

While these doctors are to be commended for their dogged attempts to discover the truth, their arguments cannot withstand scientific scrutiny. Dr. Faust is correct in noting that the studies have been done for the most part in the United States, but he ignores the important Swiss chocolate series of the Kiss Institute and the Mousse inquiries of the Academe Francais. AF As for his contention that television affects the subjects ability to respond in an unbiased manner toward the candy bar, he forgets that the images subjects respond to are not those projected by the candy company. For instance, as discussed earlier, Mr. Goodbar is loved by those who attempt to prove their prowess in sports and outdoor pursuits, yet the advertised image of Mr. Goodbar is as a friendly "fun" sort of candy bar, associated with young children and spotted dogs. Clearly, the subjects are not getting their ides from television, as Dr. Faust suggests. As for Dr. Pheelgud's allegations, just because tastes and associations change over time does not mean that there is no connection but rather that there is a connection and that it is mutable. One would not argue that fashion decisions have no ties to personality, clearly what one wears says a lot about who one is, yet these choices also change over time.

The experiments of Dr. Kaloreese and Dr. Rich show Dr. Hogg's belief regarding the relationship between candy bar choice and personality to be true. In fact, their findings serve as scientific proof for the connection. This evidence, along with one's own sense of taste as a function of persona belie the claims of skeptics and demonstrate that Hogg's words are true.

"Though many will fight me on this, and scores of others will cover their eyes and ears to ignore the knowledge I bring, I will stay on this earth loudly proclaiming what I know to be the truth: as a man lives, so does he eat, and as he chooses candy, so do we know his most private self."

OUR VERSION, WITH EDITS

Here is the version marked with the edits we thought were necessary. Are they the same as your edits? Don't worry if they aren't, but check for differences to see the reasoning behind them.

Candy Bars and Taste

ww
"preference"

Psychology has long posited a connection between the psyche and *taste* in food. The noted professor of food and psychology, *Dr.* Ima Hogg, says, "While many attempt to discover the secrets of the mind through outmoded techniques of psychoanalysis and clinical psychology, the true frontier on which we are discovering the key to personality is by assess*ment* of what people eat. Beyond this we cannot hope to go further." (WRITE IN FOOTNOTE FOR HOGG'S STUDY) Hogg's studies relating diet and psychosis went on for over twenty-five years, and they clearly show what *any* reasonable person has long suspected: *you are what you* eat. Think of the current fad of liquid diet shakes, so appropriate to our American society, *as it is* caught between the Calvinist puritanism of *its* history and the relentless greed and self-indulgence of our current market economy. Consider President Clinton and his fondness for fast food, the food of a person of action, someone ready to lead! *Or* remember the self-destructive habits of the Romans, fulfilling the slightest desire with loads of tempting delicacies, then running off to the vomitoria to rid themselves and begin again. *This* demonstrates a clear connection between what one eats and who one is. And *indeed*, the existence of a connection between food and personality points to the likelihood of a connection between candy bar choice and personality disorder.

Many studies have been done to test this theory and the results of them are here.

move to beginning of sentence

every

do not use "you"

agreement

this is in addition to—use "and" or remove entirely

All these

maybe begin the paper with this?

awk, need better transition sentence

put this later

Much has been written about ~~those~~ _extra_ candy bars that combine the various candy elements: nougat, caramel, nuts. The desire for all the things at once, the inability to make any sort of a concrete choice is typical of the boy/man who suffers from the peter pan syndrome, and the combination bar is his candy of choice. ~~This is evidenced on grounds both~~ academic and emotional. _There is both evidence_ In her ground-breaking treatise on the subject, Dr. Lotta Kaloreese interviewed a group ~~of 2,500 male~~ _this_ _unneccess._ participants between the ages of 23 and 55. Of those who said they were either ~~involved or willing to be involved in what they themselves~~ termed a "mature lifestyle," only 19.7% indicated the _lived what they_ combination bar, or "Snickers," as their primary candy choice. Of those who professed a longing to return to childhood, or to remain a child indefinitely, an astonishing 78% indicated a strong preference for the Snickers bar as their primary candy choice. (CITE KALORIES'S STUDY) Numerical results this overwhelming cannot be ignored: Snickers is the bar of ~~those who would be children forever.~~ _the eternal child_ _repetitive_

could begin with this and work up to combination

Another stunning example is the historical references of the caramel. One of the most traditional forms of confection, the caramel is the choice of those who are overly sentimental and prone to emotional outbursts and flights of fancy. Many soft-hearted artists have long called the caramel their favorite, with laudatory remarks often taking the form of song and poetry. "Boy, there's nothing a like better than a chocolate bar with caramel in it." (CHECK MLA,DO I NEED TO FOOTNOTE THIS IF I HAVE HIS NAME?) says Barry Manilow, renowned emotional person. This sort of confession is seen over and over again in memoirs of emotional people. In writings by John Denver, Sally Field, Tchaikovsky, and other softies one can find multiple references to caramel. This happens too frequently to be mere happenstance, one has yet another reason to believe that there must be some connection between the form of candy sugar that takes, and the type of person who wants that candy.

Yet another example is apparent in the strong connection between nut bars and those who love them, the tough guys both male and female. While much has been written on the connection between nuts of all types and risk-taking daredevils, including the tie between skydiving and various types of nut brittle, the clearest delineation of candy to personality is peanuts to machismo. The study was done is most particularly seen in the desire of river guides, hunters, and rock climbers for Mr. Goodbar, the peanut chocolate bar. (RICH) Dr. Rich performed his study over two years in all the venues mentioned. He used three groups among each participants. To the first group he offered a buffet table at the end of their trips which contained fruit, chocolate bars of assorted types other than Mr. Goodbars, arranged with the Mr. Goodbars at the back less reachable part of the table, with the fruit and other candy toward the front. The participants—94% of them—reached to the back to get their Mr. Goodbars. Several, 62% of those who chose the Mr. Goodbar, were heard to grunt the word "Good."

upon taking the ~~bar.~~ *candy* Dr. Rich considered the possibility that these participants had chosen the bars because they were at the back and therefore more difficult to reach and therefore a greater "prize" to these rough and tumble participants, ~~and~~ to *He used his second group* try to weed these out he set up another buffet at which the Mr. Goodbars were set near the front in easy reach, no challenge at all. Again an overwhelming majority, 86% this time, chose ~~the~~ Mr. Goodbar over any other candy. His final group was served with a mixed buffet on which the candy was arranged every which way, ~~with~~ the results *were* the same. This buffet was, in fact, picked clean of all peanut related candy, with fruit and other candy left strewn ~~apart~~ *about*, due, he hypothesizes, to the desire of "macho" individuals to hunt for their prey. On returning to his University to organize and publish his findings *Dr. Rich* he tried a control group, and offered an audience of 2,000 anthropology students the same buffet. Only an astonishing 21% chose the Mr. Goodbar, and *from a selection in which* the candy proportions were the same. [There can be no clearer evidence than this that there is indeed, a correlation between candy type and personality.] ———— *to Ⓐ a section on the next page*

should footnote this?

Scientific reason would lead one to consider whether this applied to only the nut bar, or the caramel. Recent research in the chocolate bar field has uncovered some startling findings. People who purchase ~~the~~ plain chocolate and milk chocolate bars generally complain of a feeling of a life left unfulfilled, of feelings and possibilities left unexplored. (WHOEVER)

Similar studies of randomly selected buyers of toffee bars, including the Heath and the Skor bar indicate that these buyers, or at least 89% of these buyers, can be classified as suffering from superiority complexes, defined as the strong belief that they are better than the rest of us. The compelling evidence linking the lover of coconut bars and the psychopath only cements the bond.

do not personalize

Nevertheless, There are many in both the scientific and confectionery community who protest that chocolate bar preference is merely a matter of personal taste, and hence unrelated to any personality quirks. Most notable among these groups are Dr. Faust and Dr. Pheelgud. Dr. Faust notes that much as the experiments have done to set up control groups, the studies done have not covered a wide enough expanse of the population. FOOTNOTE? OR LATER ON? In fact, all the studies, he notes, have been done in the United States where the candy bars advertise their images via television commercials. Thus it is these media images of the bars that people respond to, not the bars themselves. Dr. Pheelgud notes in his book, Candy Bars and Personality: There's No Connection, that candy bars and what goes in them changes over time, for instance licorice is not nearly as popular as it was in the early forties. PHEELGUD This change over time indicates to her that there is no real correlation, because that would indicate a change in human personality type within the space of a decade, and this she considers unlikely.

doubt the detractors

pompous? change

is

introduce him later, with his theory

companies

he maintains

another opponent of candy and personality theory,

italics

to

While these doctors are to be commended for their (dogged) attempts to discover the truth, their arguments cannot withstand scientific scrutiny. Dr. Faust is correct in noting that the studies have been done for the most part in the United States, but he ignores the important *as well as* Swiss chocolate series of the Kiss Institute, and the Mousse inquiries of the Academe Francais, AF As for his contention that television affects *need to have a sentence of explanation for what these studies are and what they show* the subjects ability to respond in an unbiased manner toward the candy bar, he forgets that the images subjects respond to are not those projected by the candy company. For instance, as discussed earlier, Mr. Goodbar is loved by those who attempt to prove their prowess in sports and outdoor pursuits, yet the advertised image of Mr. Goodbar is as a friendly "fun" sort of candy bar, associated with young children and spotted dogs. Clearly, the subjects are not getting their *a* ides from television, as Dr. Faust suggests. As for Dr. Pheelgud's allegations, just because tastes and associations change over time does not mean that —ital? *it implies,* there is no connection but rather, that there (is) a connection and that it is mutable. One would not argue that fashion decisions have no ties to personality, clearly what one wears says a lot about who one is, yet these choices also change over time.

The experiments of Dr. Kaloreese and Dr. Rich show Dr. Hogg's belief regarding the relationship between candy bar choice and *decide— personality or personality disorder* (personality) to be true. In fact, their findings serve as scientific proof for the connection. This evidence, along with one's own sense of taste as a function of persona belie the claims of skeptics and demonstrate that Hogg's words are true.

"Though many will fight me on this, and scores of others will cover *ir* the eyes and ears to ignore the knowledge I bring, I will stay on this earth loudly proclaiming what I know to be the truth: as a man lives, so does he eat, and as he chooses candy, so do we know his most private self."

Once you have made all the edits, both organizational and stylistic, you are ready to put your paper into its final stages, complete with reference and format specifications. This work is mostly mechanical, but does necessitate that you pay close attention to minute details. The end is in sight, but don't let that allow you a sloppy finish.

THE FINAL DRAFT

Sometimes You Feel Like A Nut, Sometimes You

Don't: Candy Bars and the Psychology of Taste

Psychology has long posited a connection between the psyche and food preferences. Noted professor of food and psychology Dr. Ima Hogg says, "While many attempt to discover the secrets of the mind through outmoded techniques of psychoanalysis and clinical psychology, the true frontier on which we are discovering the key to personality is an assessment of what people eat."[1] Hogg's studies relating diet and psychosis went on for over twenty-five years, and they clearly show what every reasonable person has long suspected: one is what one eats. Think of the current fad of liquid diet shakes, so appropriate to American society, caught as it is between the Calvinist puritanism of its history and the relentless greed and self-indulgence of its current market economy. Consider President Clinton and his fondness for fast food, the food of a person of action, someone ready to lead! Remember the self-destructive habits of the Romans, fulfilling the slightest desire with loads of tempting delicacies, then running off to the vomitoria to rid themselves and begin again. All these demonstrate a clear connection between what one eats and who one is. Further, the existence of a connection between food and personality points to the likelihood of a connection between candy bar choice and personality disorder.

[1] Ima Hogg, *Let's Eat Some More* (New York: Glutton & Sons, 1994), p. 107.

This theory has been tested time and time again, and the results of these tests coincide: there is a connection. One of the earliest such studies explored the historical references of the caramel. Perhaps the most traditional form of confection, the caramel is the choice of those who are overly sentimental and prone to emotional outbursts and flights of fancy. Many soft-hearted artists have long called the caramel their favorite, with laudatory remarks often taking the form of song and poetry. "Boy, there's nothing I like better than a chocolate bar with caramel in it."[2] says Barry Manilow, renowned emotional person. This sort of confession is seen over and over again in memoirs of emotional people. In writings by John Denver, Sally Field, Tchaikovsky, and other softies, one can find multiple references to caramel. This happens too frequently to be mere happenstance, yet another reason to believe that there must be some connection between the form of candy sugar takes, and the type of person who wants that candy.

Much has also been written about candy bars that combine the various candy elements: nougat, caramel, nuts. The desire for all things at once, the inability to make any sort of a concrete choice is typical of the boy/man who suffers from the Peter Pan syndrome, and the combination bar is his candy of choice. There is both academic and emotional evidence. In her ground-breaking treatise on this subject, Dr. Lotta Kaloreese interviewed 2,500 male participants between

[2] Barry Manilow, *Notes on a Sentimental Life* (Hawaii: Soft Hearts & Company, 1993) p.21.

the ages of 23 and 55. Of those who said they lived what they termed a "mature lifestyle," only 19.7% indicated the combination bar, or "Snickers," as their primary candy choice. Of those who professed a longing to return to childhood or to remain a child indefinitely, an astonishing 78% indicated a strong preference for the Snickers bar as their primary candy choice.[3] Numerical results this overwhelming cannot be ignored: Snickers is the bar of the eternal child.

Yet another example is apparent in the strong connection between nut bars and those who love them, the "tough guys," both male and female. While much has been written on the connection between nuts of all types and risk-taking daredevils, including the tie between skydiving and various types of nut brittle, the clearest instance of candy's connection to personality is the tie between peanuts and machismo. A study was commissioned to examine the common desire among river guides, hunters, and rock climbers for the Mr. Goodbar, a chocolate bar with peanuts.[4] Dr. Rich divided the participants into three groups and studied them over two years. He arranged to have a buffet table for the first group, containing fruit and chocolate bars of assorted types, including Mr. Goodbars. He designed the buffet so the Mr. Goodbars were in a remote, less reachable part of the table. The participants—94% of them—reached to the back

[3] Lotta Kaloreese, "Men Who Would Be Children" in *Experiments in Chocolate*, (Pennsylvania: Bar Press, 1991) pp. 32-45.

[4] Tu Rich, *Peanuts And Machismo* (Texas: Men Don't Press, 1993) p.10.

to get a Mr. Goodbar. Not only did this overwhelming majority select Mr. Goodbar, but 62% of those who chose the Mr. Goodbar were heard to grunt the word "Good" upon taking the candy. Dr. Rich considered the possibility that these participants had chosen the bars because they were at the back and more difficult to reach, therefore a greater "prize" to these rough-and-tumble participants. He used his second group to try to weed these out. He set up another buffet at which the Mr. Goodbars were set near the front in easy reach, no challenge at all. Again an overwhelming majority, 86% this time, chose Mr. Goodbar over any other candy. His final group was served with a mixed buffet on which the candy was arranged every which way, and the results were the same. This buffet was, in fact, picked clean of all peanut-related candy, with fruit and other candy left strewn about, due, he hypothesized, to the desire of "macho" individuals to hunt for their prey. On returning to his university to organize and publish his findings, Dr. Rich examined a control group. He offered an audience of 2,000 anthropology students the same buffet. Only 21% chose the Mr. Goodbar from a selection in which the candy proportions were the same.

Scientific curiosity would lead one to consider whether this connection between personality and preference applied only to the nut bar and the caramel. Recent research in the chocolate bar field has uncovered some startling findings. People who purchase plain chocolate and milk chocolate bars generally complain of a feeling of a life left unfulfilled, of feelings and possibilities left unexplored.[5] Similar studies of randomly selected buyers of toffee bars, including the Heath and the Skör bar, indicate that at least 89% of these buyers suffer from superiority complexes, defined as the strong belief that they are better than the rest of the population. The compelling evidence linking the lover of coconut bars and the psychopath only cements the bond. There can be no clearer evidence than this that there is, indeed, a correlation between candy type and personality.

Nevertheless, there are many in both the scientific and confectionery community who protest that chocolate bar preference is merely a matter of personal taste, and therefore unrelated to any personality quirks. Notable among these is Dr. Faust. Dr. Faust notes that, much as the experimenters have tried to set up control groups, none of the studies have covered a wide enough expanse of the population.[6] Furthermore, Dr. Faust adds, the studies have all been conducted in the United States, where the candy bar companies advertise their images via television commercials. Thus, he maintains, people in the United States respond to these media images, not to the bars themselves. Dr. Pheelgud, another opponent

[5] Hy Phat, "The Life I Could Have Had: Plain Chocolate and the Repressed" in *Watchamacallit and Aphasia: A Journal of Chocolate and Mental Health,* (Arizona: Bench Press, 1992).

[6] Goethe Faust, "I'd Sell My Soul to Publish a Book About Candy" in *Dubious Arguments Review No. 31* (New York: Hell University Press, 1990) pp. 14-23.

of candy-personality theory, notes in her book *Candy Bars and Personality: There's No Connection* that candy bars, and what goes into them, change over time. For instance licorice is not nearly as popular as it was in the early forties.[7] This change over time indicates to her that there is no real correlation, because that would indicate a change in human personality type within the space of a century, and this she considers unlikely.

While Faust and Pheelgud are to be commended for their dogged attempts to discover the truth, their arguments cannot withstand scientific scrutiny. Dr. Faust is correct in noting that the studies have been conducted for the most part in the United States, but he ignores the important Swiss chocolate series of the Kiss Institute, as well as the Mousse inquiries of the Académie francaise.[8] The Kiss Institute found the same superiority connection referred to earlier, displayed by over 500 participants from France, Switzerland, and Germany. The Mousse inquiries provided convincing evidence for the claim that various forms of mousse can be used in the treatment of many types of neuroses, establishing another clear connection between the psyche and chocolate. As for Dr. Faust's contention that television affects the subject's ability to respond in an unbiased manner toward the candy bar, he does not consider that the images projected by

[7] I. Pheelgud, *Candy Bars and Personality: There's No Connection* (New York: Skeptics & Company, 1988) pp. 34-35.
[8] Swiss Miss, *The Mousse Inquiries*

the candy company are unrelated to the interests and aspirations of the candy devotees. For instance, as discussed earlier, Mr. Goodbar is loved by those who attempt to prove their prowess in sports and outdoor pursuits, yet the advertised image of Mr. Goodbar is as a friendly "fun" sort of candy bar, associated with young children and spotted dogs. Clearly, the subjects are not getting their ideas from television, though Dr. Faust believes otherwise. As for Dr. Pheelgud's allegations, just because tastes and associations change over time does not mean that there is no connection between the two. It implies, rather, that there *is* a connection and it is mutable. One would not argue that fashion decisions have no ties to personality, clearly what one wears says a lot about who one is, yet these choices also change over time.

The experiments of Dr. Kaloreese and Dr. Rich show Dr. Hogg's belief regarding the relationship between candy bar choice and personality to be true. In fact, their findings serve as scientific proof for the connection. This evidence, along with one's own sense of taste as a function of persona, belie the claims of skeptics and demonstrate the truth of Hogg's words.

"Though many will fight me on this, and scores of others will cover their eyes and ears to ignore the knowledge I bring, I will stay on this earth loudly proclaiming what I know to be the truth: as a man lives, so does he eat, and as he chooses candy, so do we know his most private self."[9]

[9] Hogg, p.72.

Bibliography

Faust, Goethe. "I'd Sell My Soul to Publish a Book About Candy" *Dubious Arguments Review No. 31.* (1990), 14-23.

Hogg, Ima. *Let's Eat Some More.* New York: Glutton & Sons, 1994.

Kaloreese, Lotta. "Men Who Would Be Children." In *Experiments in Chocolate.* Ed. Russell Upsom Grubb. Pennsylvania: Bar Press, 1991.

Manilow, Barry. *Notes on a Sentimental Life.* Hawaii: Soft Hearts & Company, 1993.

Miss, Swiss. *The Mousse Inquiries.* Switzerland: Braids & Company, 1962.

Phat, Hy. "The Life I Could Have Had: Plain Chocolate and the Repressed." In *Watchamacallit and Aphasia: An Introduction to Chocolate and Mental Health.* Ed. Roland Butter. Arizona: Bench Press, 1992.

Pheelgud, I. *Candy Bars And Personality: There's No Connection.* New York: Skeptics & Co. 1988.

Rich, Tu. *Peanuts And Machismo: I Know They Are Connected.* Texas: Men Don't Press, 1993.

Whipt, I. M. "An Important Study." *Nougat Quarterly,* 103 (1987), 12-34.

Index

S

T

U

V

W

Y